MOUNTAIN WALKS IN GRAN CANARIA

Mountain Walks in Gran Canaria

JAVIER MARTÍNEZ GARCÍA

translated by
MICHAEL ADAMS

OPEN AIR

This book, based on
Rutas de Montaña,
Las Palmas de Gran Canaria
© Javier Martínez García 1995,
is published by Open Air,
an imprint of Four Courts Press,
Fumbally Lane, Dublin 8, Ireland
E-mail: info@four-courts-press.ie

© Javier Martínez García 1999

Maps © Justo Perez Aguado 1999

Translation © Michael Adams 1999

A catalogue record for this title
is available from the British Library.

ISBN 1-85182-349-2

Printed in Spain by
Estudios Gráficos Zure, Bilbao

Contents

Introduction

Gran Canaria is like a huge cone with its top flattened out. From that centre, many *barrancos* (ravines) extend like spokes from the centre of a wheel, to disappear into the sea. In between these ravines are areas of solid, petrified volcanic lava. The ravines and the mountains in the south and west of the island are longer and deeper than those in the north and east.

The whole island has a complex geography, and its surface is rough and gnarled. There are very few plains or plateaus: for the most part the island consists of deep ravines which spread out until they end up in the sea. This mountainous panorama must have been created millions of years ago by enormous natural forces, and the weather did the rest, with long droughts and sudden torrents which have left deep tracks down the mountainsides.

Most of our island is unknown, both to local people and visitors; very few of us have discovered how enjoyable it is to explore its hidden corners, its abandoned trails, its countless ravines and ridges, yet Gran Canaria is a wonderful example of the creative power of divine providence.

When I got the idea of describing these Walks, I thought that maybe I'd be doing nature a disservice by revealing the secrets of how to reach these mountain tops and how to negotiate the ravines: had man not done enough damage to nature? And yet there is no reason why people cannot enjoy the pleasures of the countryside *and* be sensitive to its protection and preservation.

The mountains are the last outposts of our island, the last places to be 'developed'; but all that is changing. Economic and political pressures are impacting on the last corners of our virgin territory. I think we have a duty to both our forebears and the generations to come, to do all that we can to conserve our environment.

This book is in no sense exhaustive:[1] there are hundreds of tracks it does not discuss at all. I have simply tried to provide maps and describe Walks to help the enthusiast to go 'off to the mountains' and find his way even if he does not have a great sense of direction. I want to tell the reader about places I have been to, which I have 'discovered' and spent some of the most enjoyable days of my life – out in the fresh air, in marvellous scenery, getting away from it all, and being renewed and invigorated.

[1] In fact the first edition of this book in Spanish described 50 walks. Since most English-speaking *residents* of Gran Canaria might be expected to understand a good deal of Spanish, the English edition of this book is designed for occasional visitors – most of whom are quite unaware of the island as a walkers' paradise since 'all paths lead to the beach'. But walking is a great way to take the sun, and a great way to spend a holiday (or days of it). Because the normal visitor stays quite a short while on the island, the author has selected his recommended 20 walks for this English edition.

Important Notes

• **Transport** The public bus system can, for most of the Walks, take you to the starting-point and collect you at the finishing-point. UTINSA buses cover the Northern half of the island; SALCAI buses cover the South. The list below tells you which buses suit which Walk; the bus company telephone numbers (Gran Canaria prefix 928) are: (UTINSA) 360179 and 248858; (SALCAI) 767848 and 381110.

1 BUS: UTINSA, lines 303 and 305.
2 BUS: SALCAI, lines 13 and 14.
3 BUS from Telde to Lomo Magullo: tel. no. 381110.
4 Private transport needed. (SALCAI, line 28, takes you as far as Aldea Blanca.)
5 Private transported needed.
6 BUS: SALCAI, lines 45 and 70.
7 BUS: SALCAI, lines 84 and 86.
8 Private transport needed.
9 BUS: SALCAI, line 38 and UTINSA, line 101. (There is no bus to Tasartico. You can go back to San Nicolás to get the bus home; if you do so, it means you reduce the outing to going to the beach and coming back via the Degollada del Palo and Güi Güi Chico, as described in the *Variant*).
10 BUS: SALCAI, lines 38 and 86. (Ask the driver to stop at Los Azulejos.)
11 BUS: SALCAI, line 38.
12 BUS: SALCAI, line 18. (Ask the driver to stop at the point where this road meets the road from El Juncal).
13 Private transport needed.
14 BUS: SALCAI, lines 18 and 34.
15 BUS: UTINSA: line 305. (The SALCAI, line 18 bus goes as far as the Degollada del Aserrador. You can do the whole Walk from there.)

16 BUS: UTINSA, line 101 (UTINSA, line 221 if you are doing the route from Artenara).
17 Private transport needed.
18 BUS: UTINSA, line 102.
19 BUS: UTINSA, line 305. (From Artenara, line 220.)
20 BUS: UTINSA, line 305 (to reach starting-point of Walk; get off at Lagunetas).
BUS: SALCAI, lines 18 and 34 (for the return from San Bartolomé de Tirajana).

• **Water**   Except in rainy weather, you need to bring a good supply of water because there are very few springs, and these are usually waterless during the dry season. If the water mentioned in the description of the Walk is drinkable, the author says so.

• **Footgear**   Suitable footgear is important. Boots (which give ankle support) are recommended. Special walking sandals can also be worn.

• **'Right, left'**   When reference is made to 'on the right' or 'on the left', this refers to the direction that the description of the Walk takes. But wording like 'the right-hand side' or 'the left-hand side' needs to be taken in its geographical sense i.e. with reference to the water course.

• **Litter**   The Walks described in this book are generally through areas which are fairly untouched and unlittered. So it is important not to leave any of your own litter behind you – and if possible take away any you find.

• **Estimated time**   The time given for each walk does not include an allowance for stops. If the outing includes substantial ascents, this is expressly stated. In other Walks you are told the time it would take to get to the top of a mountain from a particular point on the route, even though the time given for the Walk does not necessarily include that ascent. And, throughout, the time is calculated on the assumption that the walker is physically fit.

• **Short cuts**   Most of the routes can be shortened, and often you do not have to follow the given route to get to a mountain top. For example, you can get to the top of Cruz del Saucillo in half an hour from the main road, without having to begin your walk at San Mateo or Tenteniguada.

• **Summer heat**   Due to the intense heat and dryness of the terrain, it is not a good idea to do the Walks in the southern half of the island in the months of July, August and September. During that period the routes through Tamadaba, Pajonales and Inagua are OK: they are a bit fresher and there is shade from the pine trees.

• **A day's outing**   Each outing has been designed to be done within the one day, taking from five to eight hours. The time given is meant to be a help in planning one's outing – not a rigid target to be aimed at. By combining walks, you can plan walks which take two or more days.

• **The maps**   The maps in the book have been kept quite simple (they are not meant to be a substitute for a more elaborate ordnance maps). They are quite adequate for people who are able to 'read' maps by checking them against features of the landscape.

• **New paths**   You may find that there are new features on some of the Walks – mainly paths made since the book was written.

• **'Difficulty'**   The 'difficulty' of a Walk does not have to do with the length or the ascents and descents. It is more a matter of how clear the route is (whether or not it is easy to find your way) and whether there are any tricky bits where you have to scramble. People who are not in good physical condition will find almost all the routes hard going. You must remember that these are *mountain walks*, not Sunday afternoon family strolls. The degrees of difficulty are given as follows:

0   The whole walk uses paths or tracks, and there are no awk-
    ward or tricky bits.

1   At some stages in the walk there is no track, but it is not
    difficult to follow the route.

2   For long stretches there is no track: you need to concen-
    trate to pick up the track when it begins again; no parts are
    tricky.

3   There is a good path – and an occasional section is a little
    awkward but nothing to worry about unless you have a
    bad head for heights.

4   The path disappears at times, and there will be a section or
    two where you have to be careful.

5   There is no path and there are places where you have to be
    careful and need to scramble (but no rope work). Only
    experienced mountaineers should take on these routes.

Special Words

including Spanish words occurring in the maps

andén	a wide shelf or flat belt on a steep mountainside
aguja	*see* needle
Ascent	By 'Ascent' in the summary at the top of each Walk is meant the *total* amount of climbing involved.
barranco	ravine; perhaps the most typical feature of Canarian geography
barranquillo	a minor ravine
cairn	heap of stones (occasionally cemented together) to help you find your way
caldera	a very large crater formation, even kilometres wide
calderilla	small crater
camino real	In the Canaries this means a path (usually containing some cut stone) made by public authorities, especially in the 18th century, for public use; many of these old paths have been recently restored.
coll	a depression between two mountains; the sides can be steep or gentle; a *degollada*
degollada	*see* coll
gorge	*see barranco* [the translator has opted for 'ravine' rather than 'gorge' as the translation, and has second thoughts on discovering that the great Irish naturalist,

Robert Lloyd Praeger, in his writings on the Canaries uses 'gorge' ...]

ladera   mountainside from base to top; *laderón* if it is extensive

lomo   a gentle mountainside not involving pronounced ups and downs; usually a branch of a main mountain

llano   flat area

mesa   plateau; wide, flat area

morro   longish mountain surrounded almost completely by sheer walls

ravine   *see* barranco

risco   a vertical face, difficult or impossible to ascend

roque   a rocky prominence, normally inaccessible except by scaling; hard rock, exposed by erosion

track, etc.   track, trail, path, *camino*: almost inter-changeable

water deposits   Water at such a premium that every effort is made to conserve and control it; therefore, all these deposits bear signs of man's work.

Roque Saucillo, from San Mateo

• Ascent: 873 m. • Time: 4 hr. 30 min. • Distance: approx. 9 km. • Starting-point: San Mateo • Finishing-point: the same • Difficulty: 4

The road from San Mateo (836 m.) to Valsequillo leaves on its left the Montañón, a very typical prominence with a cross on top. Taking this road out of San Mateo, you leave it at the 39 km. mark, and take a path which brings you straight to the 43 km. mark on the same road: to begin with, the path goes past houses and then through cultivated terraces (1,084 m.–30 min.). You cross the Valsequillo road and follow a track leaving some houses and inhabited caves on your right until you get to the Lomo Chiguinique, a watershed for the Barranco de Mireles and the Barranco de Agua (from the first you can look down on La Lechucilla). The track improves and you follow a water channel until you come to a water deposit for livestock. When you have passed this, you veer right until you get to the Lomo de la Montaña Cordero, and you follow the crest until you reach a path coming from the La Lechucilla dam; you take this path left until you get to the scree (volcanic ash, *picón*) slope of the Montaña de las Arenas: you cross the scree diagonally, towards the coll which is to your left (1 hr. 15 min.). You can clearly see the track that crosses the scree. The mountain takes its name from the volcanic ash of which it is made and which you can see particularly clearly on the slope which this route follows. The geological make-up of this mountain is like that of the well-known Pico Bandama and other mountains which have expanses of similar scree on their sides.

From the coll to the top of the Montaña de la Retama (1,709 m.) there is no well defined track, but there are lots of trails made by goats and hunters. You have to go to the North-West

15

of the peak scrambling up the last twenty metres across loose scree; it is solid enough and involves no risk: however, you need a bit of experience for this (30 mins). There is an alternate route which goes round the left, to the left, following a rather overgrown path which comes out on the coll between the Retama and the Roque Saucillo.

From the Retama to the Roque Saucillo (1,690 m.) – called 'Roque' on the map – it takes you 15 min. (there is a short bit at the end which involves scrambling, but this, too, is easy enough).

For the descent you take the track which descends, to begin with, along the Barranco de Tenteniguada ; when you come to where it meets the Barranco del Agua you move onto the latter (you leave your track at a metal perimeter fence which marks off a farm, taking a path to the left which brings you down into the bottom of the ravine). Upriver you see a white-coloured structure which houses a well. Here you join up with the route you took on the ascent. To get from the top to San Mateo takes two hours.

This Walk can be changed into a comfortable two-to-three hour walk by just going up as far as the Montaña de las Arenas and beginning the route at the 43 km. mark on the road from San Mateo to Valsequillo. You cannot get lost on this route and it takes you through a typical part of the island. Since you are following the ridge for most of the Walk, you get nice views to right and left. You can see the ravine and its green slopes. This outing also has the advantage that the starting-point is very easy to get to from Las Palmas.

Los Alfaques

• Ascent: 1,050 m. • Time: 7 hr. 30 min. • Distance: approx. 15 km. • Starting-point: Tenteniguada cemetery • Finishing-point: the same • Difficulty: 0 for the Barranco de la Madre de Agua section; 3, above the Caldera de los Marteles.

You reach Tenteniguada cemetery (850 m.) via the G-814 main road from Valsequillo to San Mateo, taking the first turn left after the 48 km. mark; you are now on the Llano de los Frailes and from here you have to start walking, following the path which soon turns into a trail – the Camino de los Alfaques. This trail, they say, has as many turns as the days in the year– which is not far from the truth.

The ascent is fairly steady, but it won't exhaust you; it goes on for about one hour ten minutes in a constant zigzag along an old, very well made path, which follows the North-West slope of the Espigón (through thick vegetation); as you go, you are leaving the Barranco de la Capellanía on the right.

At 1,250 m. of altitude you reach the highest point of El Espigoñ or the Meseta de Valsequillo, an extensive plateau which separates the Barranco de la Capellanía from the Barranco de los Mocanes, where the vegetation stops. On the low part of Los Mocanes you can see the Cortijo Botija, covered with pines, and a small construction built over a waterhole in the bed of the ravine. The path runs through *piteras* (a local spikey plant) and it passes through livestock corrals on the Lomo de la Degollada de los Cardos. Higher up (20 min.) at two houses, surrounded by cultivated plots, it links up with the track which comes from Los Marteles: you have to take this track Westward (that is, to the right as you go up). After 40 mins. you reach the main Cazadores road at the Caldera de los Marteles (1,500 m.). You have to go along the road towards

17

the top for about 100 metres and then take a path to the left which meets the road beside a metal pipeline; you take this path until you come to the bed of the Barranco de la Madre de Agua. This stretch goes through a very picturesque spot covered with pines and it goes through a 50-metre tunnel which has openings on it. Just before this, there is a narrow stretch where you should go carefully because there is quite a steep drop into the ravine. When you reach the bed of the ravine you have to scramble for a little bit and then you immediately come to a cave, the Cueva del Agua, and you go on along the left slope using steps of volcanic ash and rock set into the base of the Morro de la Caldera (1,696 m.) until you come to the containing wall of the Cuevas Blancas dam or *embalsa* (1,650 m.–30 min.).

From the wall of the dam you have to go South-West towards the Degollada de los Cascajales through tilled and fallow fields; you cross a track and you come to another track a little higher up which runs from the main road to Los Pechos. At Los Cascajales you leave the track and ascend (there is no path) by the East slope of the Calderilla until you reach its highest point (1,840 m.–39 min.); from here you can see the round form of the crater, following the watershed until you reach the Roque Redondo aerials. You then go on, leaving on your left the dense pine wood, and you keep to the protective fence going towards the Pico de los Nieves, and then you immediately reach the main road which links the aerials with the Pico (45 min.).

For the descent you can go back the way you came, as far as the Caldera de los Marteles, and there you take the track which goes North: you stay on it all the way, and, when it comes to an end, it becomes a trail which goes past a spring and the base of the Roque Grande. When you get to the first houses of El Rincón, you take a path which goes down through cultivated fields until you get to a water deposit situated in the bed of the Barranco de la Capellanía; you then follow the pipeline from this deposit (keep to the right of it) until you come to the start of the Los Afaques road and the place where you started out from (3 hr. 30 min.)

This ascent can be combined with a descent to Santa Lucía along the road between the Mesa de las Vacas and Las Vueltas de Taidía.

Barranco de los Cernícalos

• Ascent: 800 m. • Time: 3 hr. 35 min. • Distance: approx. 6 km. • Starting-point: Bottom of the ravine: on the road from Telde to Lomo Magullo, when you reach the Los Arenales cross-roads you take the turn right which brings you to the bottom of the ravine • Finishing-point: Cazadores • Difficulty: 0

The Barranco de los Cernícalos is one of the three on the island through which water flows freely all the year round: this is its great feature, one we hope it will never lose, because it accounts for the dense, unique vegetation covering the entire bed of the ravine – tall wild olive-trees and Canarian willows, a wonderful natural heritage.

The route starts off in the very bed of the ravine; you go up along a short cement track until you reach some houses. A little further down, the ravine joins the Barranco de la Breña, at which point the two ravines lose their identity and become the Barranco de San Miguel.

For the first ten minutes of the walk you don't see the water because it is in a channel, but the channel soon stops and then you see water free-flowing from its source. The path is still quite clear (sometimes it is on the right of the flow, sometimes on the left) until you reach an area of overgrown plots beside a derelict shed and a very big wild olive-tree (50 min.); before you reach this, you pass a small waterfall. About 25 minutes further on, you reach a second waterfall where the water falls almost vertically for a few metres. A kilometre further on the river narrows into a spectacular ravine, with vertical walls 30 metres high on both sides, at the end of which you meet another waterfall (15 min.–720 m.). This is the most scenic part of the route: so many kestrels (*cernícalos*) are to be found on these cliffs that this bird of prey has given its name to the entire ravine.

The ravine comes to a dead end; you have to retrace your steps and take a path which goes South, parts company with the channel and rises steeply to 900 metres, at which point you meet a track which comes off the Cazadores road. This route passes a big cave used as shelter for livestock. (An alternative, though it is much longer and complicated, is to take another path which leads out of the channel and, going up the opposite side, avoids the cliff and the tunnel mentioned below.)

The track takes you to a structure built over a water deposit and a tunnel (50 min.) from which runs a small channel of water which feeds into the main channel; this area is known as 'Los Guinderos'. The track disappears and becomes a trail which runs parallel to the river, crossing it at three points until it reaches the water tunnel from which the main stream springs (45 min.–1,150 m.). A bit above that, you come to a white cave and below it a house to which a track runs from Cazadores; you follow this track until you reach that village 30 minutes later (1,250 m.).

Though not included in this walk, you can follow the gorge upwards (there is no stream from here on), until you reach the Caldera de los Marteles – but it is not an easy walk because there is no well defined path and there is dense undergrowth (mostly *tuneras*, a type of cactus).

Amurga, from Aldea Blanca

• *Ascent: 711 m.* • *Time: 5 hr. 20 min.* • *Distance: approx 9 km.* • *Starting-point: Gallegos, at a point 5.5 km. from Aldea Tirajana, along a track that runs parallel to the right-hand side of the ravine. The track begins on the left of the town football field as you go West.* • *Finishing-point: the same* • *Difficulty: 1.*

At a point 5.5 km. from Aldea Blanca you reach the bed of the Barranquillo de Gallegos (420 m.) where there are some derelict houses and a magnificent palm-tree. The track is designed for 4-wheel-drive vehicles, but it can be used by ordinary cars if driven carefully.

To the left of the bed of the gorge a path starts which brings you to a small man-made pool, and a spring a few metres above it (there is always water there). You keep going, leaving a big cypress on your left, and you pass by some ruined cottages; the track then parts company with the ravine bed and heads straight towards the saddle. It then goes alongside the bed again and then it leaves it and goes up the side of the ravine. You reach the coll (734 m.) in one hour, leaving the Roque de la Vuelta on your left; at the top of this Roque there is a house built for use during construction work on the small dam on the Barranco de Las Palmas: from the top of the Roque the material used in the construction was sent down a chute designed for that purpose. The track that takes you to this house begins very near Aldea Blanca and is impassable to vehicles: it is a nice walk for people who don't want to do anything very strenuous.

At the coll you turn right, following a track which runs below the rocks and goes diagonally upwards to the higher slope. The path runs out at some point, but you find it again

22

below the crest from which you can look down into the Barranco de Tirajana. You come to a stretch where you have to keep to the right; when this stretch ends, you go cross-country on the right-hand slope until you reach Amurga (1,131 m.– 2 hr.).

Amurga is shaped like a huge prow from which you can see on the right the Barranco de Tirajana, in the bed of which (800 m. below) you can see the dam, La Fortaleza, La Sorrueda, San Bartolomé and, to the left, the Barranco de Fataga and the village that bears its name. This 'prow' continues, losing height along the Lomo de los Pajarcillos (or Cumbrecillas de Amurga) which is not so much a ridge as a succession of big rocky outcrops in the Fataga direction – the Roque de la Sabina, Los Gánigos and other lesser ones. There are some pine trees which literally grow out over the ravine.

Going South you come in 20 minutes to the Roque Almeida (also known as Talayón or Moño Mujeres: 1,107 m.), a feature easily visible from the Fataga–Maspalomas road; it is an easy ascent and well worth doing because the sheer drop into the ravine, the West face, is very spectacular. Between the two peaks there are some stone houses in ruins, which were formerly shelters used by goatherds.

You go back by the track which takes you past a white cross set up as a memorial to FPDR, who died on 23 October 1981; when you reach the point where the track forks, you go to the left; this brings you down towards the Barranco de Tirajana passing alongside a cave-dwelling and (1 hr. 10 min. on) it links up with the track running down through the ravine. You continue along this track going to the right, to Aldea Blanca, which brings you to your original starting-point in Gallegos in 20 minutes.

With the exception of the Palmera de Gallegos and a few pines on the very top, you don't meet a single tree in the entire course of this walk. The whole Amurga mountain complex is located in the South East of the island, where there is very little rainfall: the landscape is almost lunar – dry, desert, typical of the southern area. Only very resilient plants such as *salvias, tomillos, tabaibas, bejeques, veroles,* and *cardones* can survive in this sort of setting. You will meet some colonies of *cardoncillos*, a plant in danger of extinction, with its characteristic form of a silver candelabra branching in all directions.

I recommend this as a Spring outing or one to do a few days after there has been rain, which is when it is at its greenest and most colourful: better not to do it at other times, when it can be really very hot. This route can be combined with a descent to Fataga along the coll near Roque Talayón or a descent towards Maspalomas as far as the Degollada de la Yegua.

(12 miles?)

Montaña Negra and Pilancones

• *Ascent: 735 m.* • *Time: 4 hr. 30 min.* • *Distance: approx. 12 km.* • *Starting-point: the Gambuesa dam, at Ayaguares* • *Finishing-point: the same* • *Difficulty: 0.*

The Gambuesa dam (340 m.) is above the Ayaguares dam, in the townland of Ayagaures; both dams collect the water which drains off the huge Pilancones circle via the Barranco de la Data. You cross the wall of the Gambuesa dam on which runs the 'Trasvasur' pipeline (as yet unfinished, this will pipe water from the Soria dam to Las Palmas). You immediately come to the Casas (houses) de Ayagaures Alta, which are set among palm trees. Your route starts up the path which is just above the highest-up house; it has the numbers 37 and 85 on its gate; you follow the path for about five minutes until you come to a (permanent) spring.

The route continues North and slowly ascends the Western flank of the mountain which acts as a watershed with the Vicentes ravine; it goes through pines and brings you very close to the Punta de los Artajos (641 m.) which it leaves on its right. This Punta is very easy to see because it has white sheer walls and lots of caves; if you look down you can see the Casas de Taginastal, in the bottom of the ravine. On the opposite side, closing off the ravine on the West, are the prominences of Montaña del Rey and Montaña Alta (or M. de la Sabinilla), 960 and 1,062 m. respectively. Further up, the path crosses the shoulder of the Cumbre de Trujillo, leaves on its left a derelict house with a red roof, and links up with a forestry track; you follow this track upwards until you come to a cement pool (950 m.–2 hr.): to the left lies Montaña Negra (1,075 m.) which you can ascend and descend easily in 30 minutes. Staying on the track for another kilometre you meet the recently restored

25

path made for the descent to Pino Pilancones (15 min.). This path comes from the Degollada de Manzanilla and San Bartolomé de Tirajana and it is very easy from here to see Pilancones (a further 20 min. on). At first there is a very steep bit, until you reach the bottom of the Barranco de la Cisterna.

Pino Pilancones gives its name to the Pilancones-Ayagaures nature reserve, an enormous crater (formed by erosion) in which is located one of the most southerly pine forests on the island. All accesses to this area are blocked to traffic to stop the steady deterioration of the environment.

From Pilancones the route continues in the direction of Las Tederas (30 min.), a picturesque spot dotted with some houses set among fruit trees and ancient palm trees; on the highest point of the stretch you pass the Descansadero de los Muertos, a stone table with a cross and a plaque which explains why it's there.

At Las Tederas you take the track which will bring you to the dams in 55 minutes. This whole route can be done the reverse way, starting your walk in Las Tederas, or combining the walk with routes into the Pino from San Bartolomé de Tirajana (via the Degollada de Manzanilla) or from the Degollada de Cruz Grande, on the road towards Ayacata. If you do in fact start your walk at Las Tederas, you will reach the Pino in 45 minutes: this is the quickest and shortest of the four ways to the Pino, though the track to Las Tederas is not in a very good state of repair.

Morro de Hierba Huerto

• Ascent: 834 m. • Time: 7 hr. • Distance: approx. 8 km. • Starting-point: the Mirador del Lomo del Palmito on the road from Maspalomas to Ayagaures via Montaña La Data and Monte León • Finishing-point: the same • Difficulty: 0

The route begins at the Mirador (a vantage-point, with parking at 485 m.) from which you can see Ayaguares (North-East) and Palmitos Park (West). You take the track up the Lomo del Palmito which starts beside a house which you leave on your right. The track ends above a group of houses at a hole made for a small reservoir. You have to go through a gate in a metal fence and through another gate higher up, at which point the track ends and a trail begins. You ascend parallel to the bed of the Barranco del Palmito along its left side, very soon crossing to the right and going up the slope in a zig-zag until you come to a mountain which is a watershed with a minor ravine which is a tributary of the Barranco del Palmito. The route is marked by small cairns and you easily reach a forestry track (890 m.–1 hr. 40 min.). Before this, at the point when you are able to see the Barranco de Chamoriscán, the track divides in two and you have to go to the right because the other track leads off to some houses on the bed of the ravine.

The forestry track ends between the Montaña Alta and the Montaña del Rey on the East, and you keep going on it for 25 minutes until you reach the Degollada de los Helechos (908 m.), at which point you follow the obvious route along the Lomo de los Helechos until you come to a big conical marker where the trail divides in two (20 min.): on your way back you will descend the trail that goes straight on, but now you have to take the one that goes up left along the side of the Barranco de Chamoriscán. A bit further on it forks again: if you take the

27

left, you go into the bed of the ravine and find the track from Tablero de Maspalomas to Chira, but you *don't* go left; you go right – up to the Degollada de Hierba Huerto (1,226 m.–35 min.) from where you can see the Chira dam and from which another track (to the right) takes you to the summit (1,1319 m.–15 min.). The view from this unique vantage-point is quite spectacular.

You make your descent by going back along the track to the Degollada de Hierba Huerto and from there along the trail on the side of the Barranco de Chira (opposite to what you did coming up) which loses height rapidly until it meets the restored path which goes North-East towards the Degollada del Dinero and the Degollada de Cruz Grande. When you reach the Degollada del Sordo (1,115 m.–50 min.) you leave the main path and take the path to the left which is a spectacular section of the Walk, exposed but safe, along the East face of the huge bulk of the Hierba Huerto and the Montaña de las Tortolas. To the East you can see the Pino Pilancones, above Las Tederas, whose bulk stands out above all the surrounding pines. You go through some wet stretches of ground covered with rushes; there is a spring just below the third group of rushes (you scarcely have to leave the path to reach it). The trail passes by the conical marker you saw on the way up (50 min.) and the Degollada de los Helechos, and from here on you go back along the same route as you came up, reaching your starting-point in 2 hr. 5 min.

There is an alternate way of going back from the Degollada de los Helechos. It descends to Las Tederas by a very uncared-for path; from Las Tederas to Ayagaures along 5 km. of track (see Walk No. 5); and from Ayagaures to the Lomo del Palmito by 3.2 km. of tarmac road; but it is a pretty long walk and you lose 250 m. of height to get down to Ayagaures and then you have to make it up again on the tarmac.

This Walk can be combined with entering the Pilancones circle via Cruz Grande and the Degollada del Dinero, and ending up in San Bartolomé via the Degollada de Manzanilla, or in Cercados de Araña via the Chira dam.

Montaña de Tauro

• *Ascent: 1,114 m.* • *Time: 6 hr. 30 min.* • *Distance: approx. 17 km.* • *Starting-point: El Cercado, on the road from Puerto Mogán to Mogán, two km. from where it crosses the Las Palmas road.* • *Finishing point: Mogán* • *Difficulty: 1*

The Montaña de Tauro has the form of a truncated pyramid, with a huge plateau on top from where you get a bird's-eye view of the entire South-West of the island. The Inagua and Sándara massifs have no vantage-point to compare with this; here you can see the entire ridge from West to East. To the North-East lies the Soria dam and to the North Las Niñas dam.

The route follows a SW to N direction, just like the Barranco de Mogán which it parallels. It is a linear route almost the whole way.

El Cercado (100 m.) is a small section of Mogán on the left hand side of the gorge; here are grown the vegetables and fruit for which it is famous. Inside the village there is a little turn to the left: where the tarmac stops you have to start your walk by taking a short track leading to cultivated terraces; at the fork you take the track to the left and when this stops you have to go up the slope, right, beside a cairn of stones and parallel to a derelict irrigation channel. You immediately reach the splendid bridle path which ascends by the left-hand side of the Hoya del Salitre, a route flanked by huge *tabaibas* (a common local shrub). Almost at the end of the Hoya the path crosses to the other side, passes by a disused waterpipe and continues via the bed of the Cañada (open ravine) de los Parados. The path through the bottom of this Cañada divides in two; you have to go to the right, ascending until you find a path which leads you to the top of the Lomo del Taurito (on the other side is the ravine of that name). From this point onwards, until the end, your track appears and disappears: sometimes it is excellent, sometimes there is no sign of it.

When you reach the upper part of the Cañada, the landscape is desolate and yet spectacular, a mixture of shrubs and thousands of heaps of stones made by people when clearing the ground for cultivation. It is a long time since any harvest was won here, but you cannot help being impressed by the effort people made to scratch a living in times of scarcity (in years when there was rainfall). These piles of stones bear silent witness to those hard times. The route has already entered the Llanos del Guirre leaving the Laderones (748 m.–1 hr. 30 min.) on its left and running close to the clefts which allow you to peer down into the ravine.

You reach El Guirre (932 m.) in another 30 minutes (opposite it is Mogán, which lies 680 metres below). This is a key triangulation point and so it has a large white cylinder set on a quadrangular base. Before you reach El Guirre, on its southern slope there is a spring beside the path; above the spring, in the Western part of the Guirre rocks, there is an excellent cave, fairly clean, which can accommodate ten or twelve people. To the right you pass a small wood of stately pines called 'Piñitos Nuevos'.

From El Guirre you carry on North along the ridge leaving the Andenes de la Hoya de Almacigo on your left: these are sheer shelfed walls which drop right down into the ravine, upwater from Mogán. You keep on the path until you reach a two-roomed semi-derelict house used as a base for reafforestation. Up against the house there is a line of transplanted *cardoncillos* (a low plant, with a characteristic form of a silver candelabra) and you reach here in 30 minutes. The path goes on, upwards, to the right of the house, and will take you all the way to the top of the Montaña de Tauro (1,214 m.–1 hr.). If, when you reach the house you take the path which keeps going right, you will come to the Degollada de las Lapas from which you will be able to see the deep Barranco de Tauro and, further to the East, that of the Barranco de Arguineguín.

Through the Barranco de Tauro there runs a good bridlepath which leads to the Morro de los Majanos.

The descent is by the same route, and it takes three hours to get to Mogán via Laderones.

You can also, if you wish, stay on the well-made path (*camino real*) which you came up on and which goes round the West side of Tauro (this is called the Swedish Route) and descends to the road on the small Andrés ravine which links up with the track from Ayacata to Mogán, very close to the Mulato dam. This descent takes longer and involves seven kms. by track and tarmac to take you to Mogán.

Barranco de Chira

• Ascent: 700 m. • Time: 6 hr. 5 min. • Length: approx. 12 km.
• Starting-point: the Barranco de Arguineguín road. After pass-
ing Cercados de Espino going towards Soria, you leave the
main road 3 km. on and take the turn to the right which fol-
lows the channel of the ravine heading for La Solana. About
600 metres after the turn you leave your vehicle at the point
where the Barranco de Soria meets the Barranco de Arguine-
guín • Finishing-point: the same. • Difficulty: 1.

The point (250 m.) where the Barranco de Chira meets the
Barranco de Arguineguín (an offshoot of it) is clear to see.
There are two earthen tracks, one on each side of the Barranco
de Chira: you must take the one on the right (on the left hand
side of the ravine) which takes you past some houses and water deposits and goes gradually up the side of the ravine until
it crosses the channel on to the other side, where it begins to
get steep; after taking a few twists it brings you to the open
ground of Huesa Bermeja. You should not follow the branch
which goes off to the right, down towards the Casas (houses)
de El Brusco. Nor should you go off, higher on the right, towards the houses of Huesa Bermeja: you stay on the main
track until you come to a little flat area, at which point you
have to follow the branch right, where the track is crossed by
a pipeline (600 m.–1 hr. 10 min.). (The branch left would take
you to the tunnel in the channel of the Soria dam.) We are now
at the Southern base of the Montañón, a huge spur whose sheer
sides drop down into the Barranco de Chira. To the South the
ravine opens out and you can see the right-hand flank of the
Barranco de Arguineguín and the Degollada de Cortadores,
the Punta Gavilanes and the narrow serpentine road which leads
to Soria.

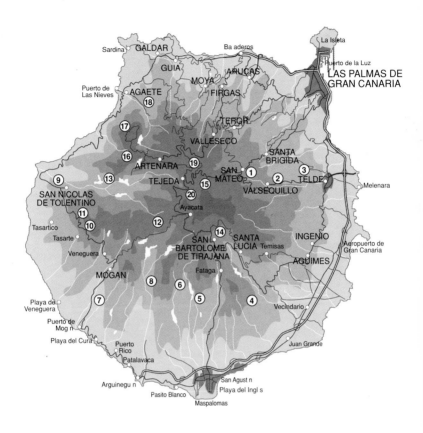

Map of Gran Canaria
showing the location of the walks

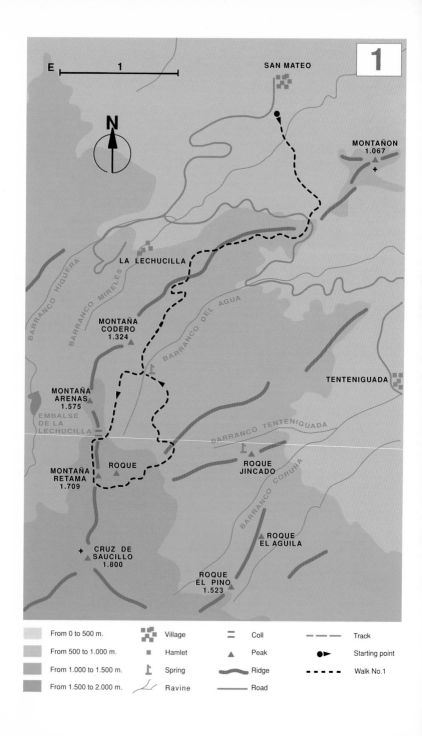

E |———— 1 ————|

N

1

SAN MATEO

MONTAÑON
1.067

LA LECHUCILLA

BARRANCO HIGUERA

BARRANCO MIRELES

BARRANCO DEL AGUA

MONTAÑA
CODERO
1.324

TENTENIGUADA

MONTAÑA
ARENAS
1.575

EMBALSE
DE LA
LECHUCILLA

BARRANCO TENTENIGUADA

BARRANCO CORUÑA

ROQUE

ROQUE
JINCADO

MONTAÑA
RETAMA
1.709

ROQUE
EL AGUILA

CRUZ DE
SAUCILLO
1.800

ROQUE
EL PINO
1.523

From 0 to 500 m.	Village	Coll	Track
From 500 to 1.000 m.	Hamlet	Peak	Starting point
From 1.000 to 1.500 m.	Spring	Ridge	Walk No.1
From 1.500 to 2.000 m.	Ravine	Road	

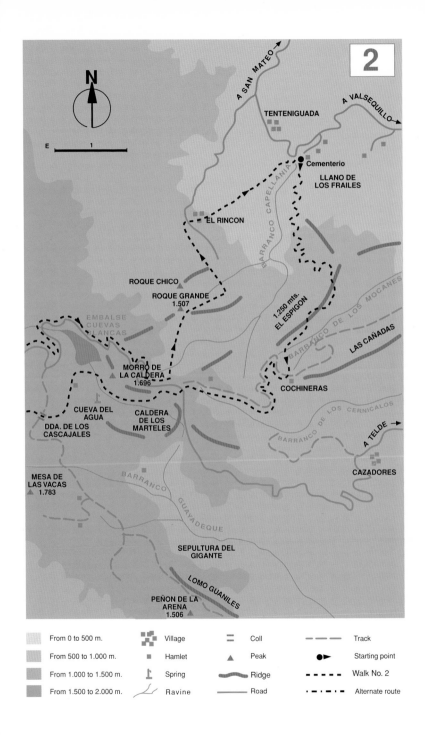

2

N

E   1

A SAN MATEO

A VALSEQUILLO

TENTENIGUADA

Cementerio

LLANO DE
LOS FRAILES

BARRANCO CAPELLANIA

EL RINCON

ROQUE CHICO

ROQUE GRANDE
1.507

1.250 mts.
EL ESPIGON

BARRANCO DE LOS MOCANES

LAS CAÑADAS

EMBALSE
CUEVAS
BLANCAS

MORRO DE
LA CALDERA
1.696

BARRANCO DE LOS CERNICALOS

COCHINERAS

CUEVA DEL
AGUA

CALDERA
DE LOS
MARTELES

A TELDE

DDA. DE LOS
CASCAJALES

BARRANCO DE LOS CERNICALOS

CAZADORES

MESA DE
LAS VACAS
1.783

BARRANCO

GUAYADEQUE

SEPULTURA DEL
GIGANTE

LOMO GUANILES

PEÑON DE LA
ARENA
1.506

From 0 to 500 m.	Village	Coll	Track
From 500 to 1.000 m.	Hamlet	Peak	Starting point
From 1.000 to 1.500 m.	Spring	Ridge	Walk No. 2
From 1.500 to 2.000 m.	Ravine	Road	Alternate route

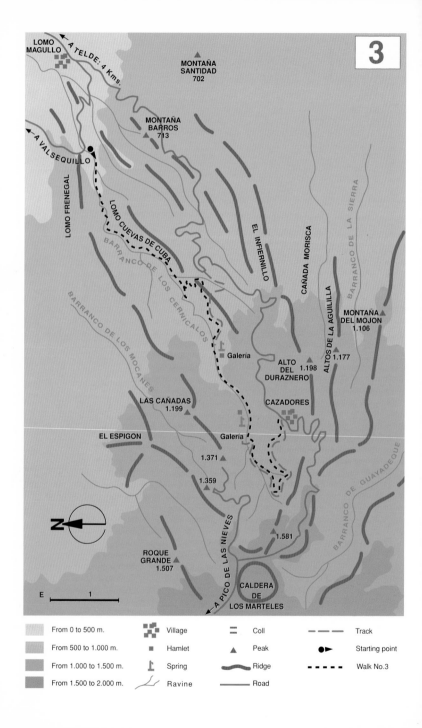

3

LOMO
MAGULLO

A TELDE: 4 Kms.

MONTAÑA
SANTIDAD
702

A VALSEQUILLO

MONTAÑA
BARROS
713

LOMO FRENEGAL

LOMO CUEVAS DE CUBA

EL INFIERNILLO

CAÑADA MORISCA

BARRANCO DE LA SIERRA

BARRANCO DE LOS CERNICALOS

BARRANCO DE LOS MOCANES

MONTAÑA
DEL MOJON
1.106

ALTOS DE LA AGUILILLA

1.177

Galería

ALTO
DEL
DURAZNERO
1.198

LAS CAÑADAS
1.199

CAZADORES

EL ESPIGON

Galería

BARRANCO DE GUAYADEQUE

1.371

1.359

A PICO DE LAS NIEVES

1.581

ROQUE
GRANDE
1.507

CALDERA
DE
LOS MARTELES

N

E   1

From 0 to 500 m.	Village	Coll	Track
From 500 to 1.000 m.	Hamlet	Peak	Starting point
From 1.000 to 1.500 m.	Spring	Ridge	Walk No.3
From 1.500 to 2.000 m.	Ravine	Road	

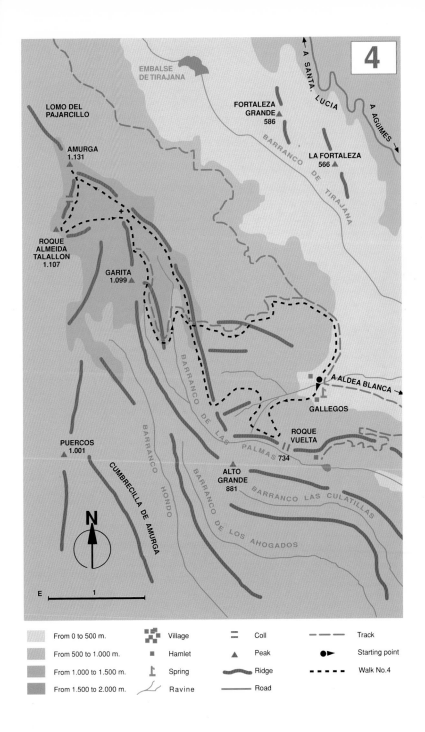

4

EMBALSE
DE TIRAJANA

A SANTA LUCIA

A AGÜIMES →

LOMO DEL
PAJARCILLO

FORTALEZA
GRANDE
586

LA FORTALEZA
566

AMURGA
1.131

BARRANCO DE TIRAJANA

ROQUE
ALMEIDA
TALALLON
1.107

GARITA
1.099

BARRANCO DE LAS

A ALDEA BLANCA →

GALLEGOS

ROQUE
VUELTA

PALMAS 734

PUERCOS
1.001

BARRANCO HONDO

CUMBRECILLA DE AMURGA

ALTO
GRANDE
881

BARRANCO LAS CULATILLAS

BARRANCO DE LOS AHOGADOS

N

E   1

From 0 to 500 m.	Village	Coll	Track
From 500 to 1.000 m.	Hamlet	Peak	Starting point
From 1.000 to 1.500 m.	Spring	Ridge	Walk No.4
From 1.500 to 2.000 m.	Ravine	Road	

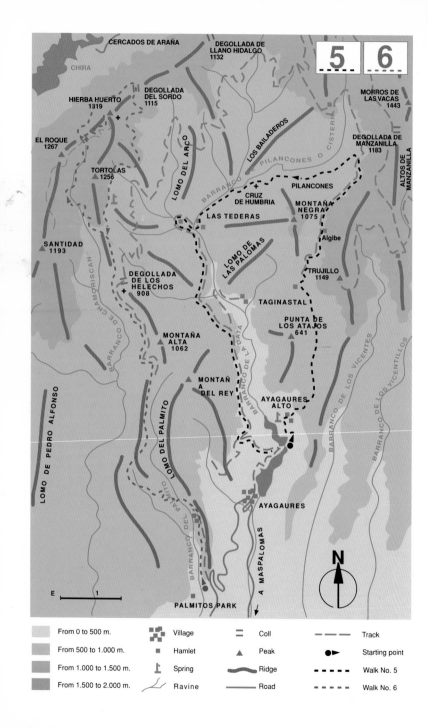

CERCADOS DE ARAÑA

DEGOLLADA DE
LLANO HIDALGO
1132

CHIRA

DEGOLLADA
DEL SORDO
1115

HIERBA HUERTO
1319

MORROS DE
LAS VACAS
1443

EL ROQUE
1267

DEGOLLADA DE
MANZANILLA
1183

TORTOLAS
1256

ALTOS DE
MANZANILLA

LOS BAILADEROS

PILANCONES O CISTERN

PILANCONES

CRUZ
DE HUMBRIA

MONTAÑA
NEGRA
1075

LOMO DEL ARCO

BARRANCO

LAS TEDERAS

SANTIDAD
1193

Algibe

LOMO DE
LAS PALOMAS

BARRANCO DE CHAMORISCAN

DEGOLLADA
DE LOS
HELECHOS
908

TRUJILLO
1149

TAGINASTAL

PUNTA DE
LOS ATAJOS
641

MONTAÑA
ALTA
1062

BARRANCO DE LA DATA

BARRANCO DE LOS VICENTES

BARRANCO DE LOS VICENTILLOS

MONTAÑA
DEL REY

AYAGAURES
ALTO

LOMO DE PEDRO ALFONSO

LOMO DEL PALMITO

BARRANCO DEL PALMITO

AYAGAURES

A MASPALOMAS

E   1

N

PALMITOS PARK

From 0 to 500 m.	Village	Coll	Track
From 500 to 1.000 m.	Hamlet	Peak	Starting point
From 1.000 to 1.500 m.	Spring	Ridge	Walk No. 5
From 1.500 to 2.000 m.	Ravine	Road	Walk No. 6

5 6

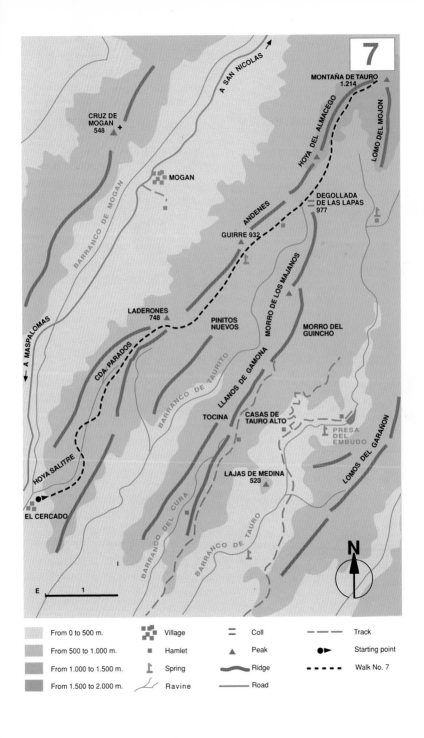

7

A SAN NICOLAS

MONTAÑA DE TAURO
1.214

CRUZ DE
MOGAN
548

LOMO DEL MOJON

HOYA DEL ALMACEGO

MOGAN

ANDENES

DEGOLLADA
DE LAS LAPAS
977

BARRANCO DE MOGAN

GUIRRE 932

MORRO DE LOS MAJANOS

A MASPALOMAS

LADERONES
748

PINITOS
NUEVOS

MORRO DEL
GUINCHO

CDA. PARADOS

BARRANCO DE TAURITO

LLANOS DE GAMONA

TOCINA

CASAS DE
TAURO ALTO

PRESA
DEL
EMBUDO

LOMOS DEL GARAÑON

HOYA SALITRE

LAJAS DE MEDINA
523

EL CERCADO

BARRANCO DEL CURA

BARRANCO DE TAURO

N

E   1

░░ From 0 to 500 m.	Village	Coll	Track
▒▒ From 500 to 1.000 m.	Hamlet	Peak	Starting point
▓▓ From 1.000 to 1.500 m.	Spring	Ridge	Walk No. 7
██ From 1.500 to 2.000 m.	Ravine	Road	

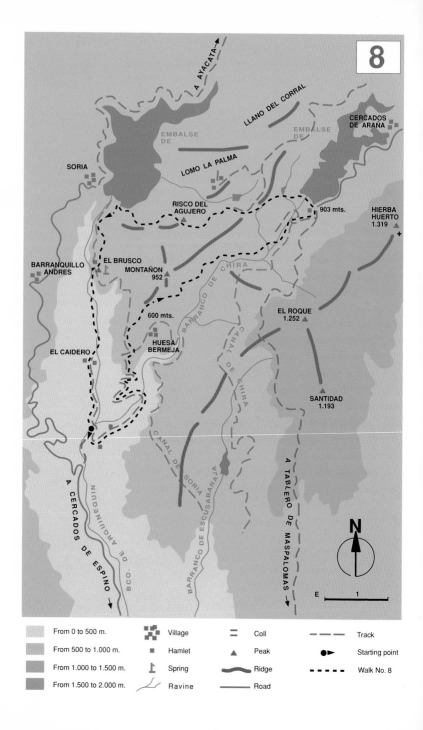

8

A AYACATA

LLANO DEL CORRAL

EMBALSE DE

CERCADOS DE ARANA

EMBALSE DE

SORIA

LOMO LA PALMA

RISCO DEL AGUJERO

903 mts.

HIERBA HUERTO 1.319

BARRANQUILLO ANDRES

EL BRUSCO MONTAÑON 952

BARRANCO DE CHIRA

EL ROQUE 1.252

600 mts.

EL CAIDERO

HUESA BERMEJA

CANAL DE CHIRA

SANTIDAD 1.193

CANAL DE SORIA

A TABLERO DE MASPALOMAS

A CERCADOS DE ESPINO

BCO. DE ARGUINEGUIN

BARRANCO DE ESCUSABARAJA

N

E _____ 1

▓ From 0 to 500 m.	🏘	Village	═	Coll	– – – Track
▓ From 500 to 1.000 m.	▪	Hamlet	▲	Peak	●► Starting point
▓ From 1.000 to 1.500 m.	🌱	Spring	▬	Ridge	▪ ▪ ▪ Walk No. 8
▓ From 1.500 to 2.000 m.	〰	Ravine	──	Road	

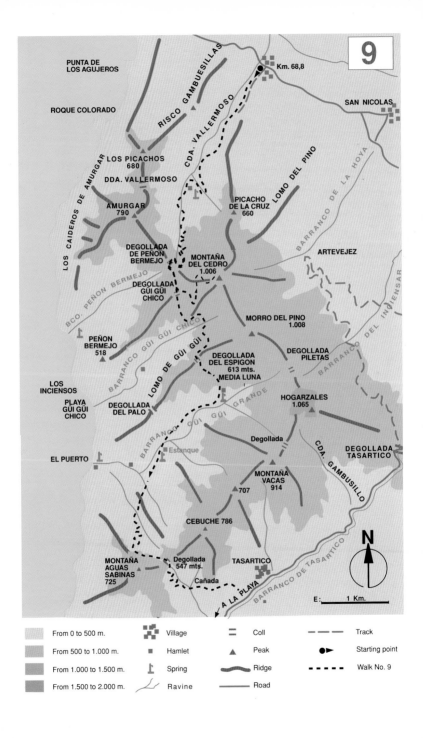

9

PUNTA DE
LOS AGUJEROS

Km. 68,8

SAN NICOLAS

ROQUE COLORADO

RISCO GAMBUESILLAS

CDA. VALLERMOSO

LOS PICACHOS
680

DDA. VALLERMOSO

LOMO DEL PINO

BARRANCO DE LA HOYA

LOS CAIDEROS DE AMURGAR

AMURGAR
790

PICACHO
DE LA CRUZ
660

ARTEVEJEZ

DEGOLLADA
DE PEÑON
BERMEJO

MONTAÑA
DEL CEDRO
1.006

DEGOLLADA
GÜI GÜI
CHICO

BCO. PEÑON BERMEJO

PEÑON
BERMEJO
518

MORRO DEL PINO
1.008

BARRANCO DEL INDIENSAR

DEGOLLADA
DEL ESPIGON
613 mts.

DEGOLLADA
PILETAS

LOMO DE GÜI GÜI

BARRANCO GÜI GÜI CHICO

MEDIA LUNA

LOS
INCIENSOS

PLAYA
GÜI GÜI
CHICO

DEGOLLADA
DEL PALO

GÜI GÜI GRANDE

HOGARZALES
1.065

CDA. GAMBUSILLO

DEGOLLADA
TASARTICO

EL PUERTO

BARRANCO

Estanque

Degollada

MONTAÑA
VACAS
914

707

CEBUCHE 786

MONTAÑA
AGUAS
SABINAS
725

Degollada
547 mts.

TASARTICO

BARRANCO DE TASARTICO

Cañada

A LA PLAYA

N

E: 1 Km.

From 0 to 500 m.   Village   Coll   Track

From 500 to 1.000 m.   Hamlet   Peak   Starting point

From 1.000 to 1.500 m.   Spring   Ridge   Walk No. 9

From 1.500 to 2.000 m.   Ravine   Road

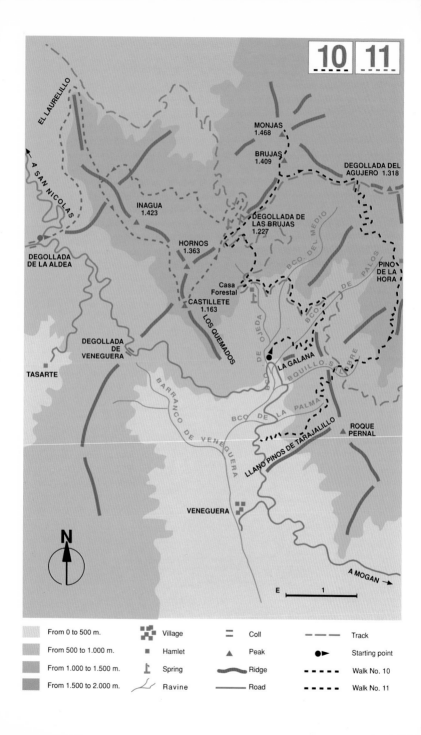

EL LAURELILLO

A SAN NICOLAS

MONJAS
1.468

BRUJAS
1.409

DEGOLLADA DEL
AGUJERO 1.318

INAGUA
1.423

DEGOLLADA DE
LAS BRUJAS
1.227

BCO. DEL MEDIO

HORNOS
1.363

PINO
DE LA
HORA

DEGOLLADA
DE LA ALDEA

Casa
Forestal

BCO. DE PALOS

CASTILLETE
1.163

BCO. DE OJEDA

LOS QUEMADOS

LA GALANA

DEGOLLADA
DE
VENEGUERA

BOQUILLO-S

BCO. DE LA LIEBRE

TASARTE

BARRANCO

BCO. DE LA PALMA

ROQUE
PERNAL

DE

VENEGUERA

LLANO PINOS DE TARAJALILLO

VENEGUERA

N

A MOGAN →

E   1

From 0 to 500 m.

Village

Coll

Track

From 500 to 1.000 m.

Hamlet

Peak

Starting point

From 1.000 to 1.500 m.

Spring

Ridge

Walk No. 10

From 1.500 to 2.000 m.

Ravine

Road

Walk No. 11

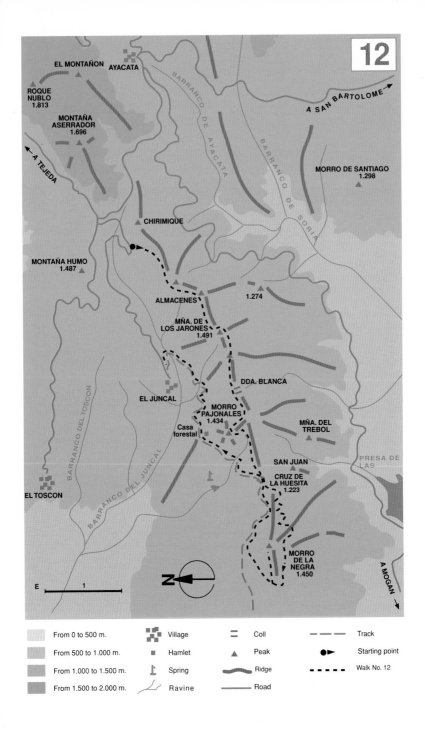

12

EL MONTAÑON   AYACATA

ROQUE
NUBLO
1.813

MONTAÑA
ASERRADOR
1.696

A TEJEDA

BARRANCO DE AYACATA

BARRANCO DE SORIA

A SAN BARTOLOME

MORRO DE SANTIAGO
1.298

CHIRIMIQUE

MONTAÑA HUMO
1.487

ALMACENES

1.274

MÑA. DE
LOS JARONES
1.491

BARRANCO DEL TOSCON

EL JUNCAL

DDA. BLANCA

MORRO
PAJONALES
1.434

MÑA. DEL
TREBOL

Casa
forestal

BARRANCO DEL JUNCAL

SAN JUAN

CRUZ DE
LA HUESITA
1.223

PRESA DE
LAS

EL TOSCON

MORRO
DE LA
NEGRA
1.450

A MOGAN

N

E   1

From 0 to 500 m.	Village	Coll	Track
From 500 to 1.000 m.	Hamlet	Peak	Starting point
From 1.000 to 1.500 m.	Spring	Ridge	Walk No. 12
From 1.500 to 2.000 m.	Ravine	Road	

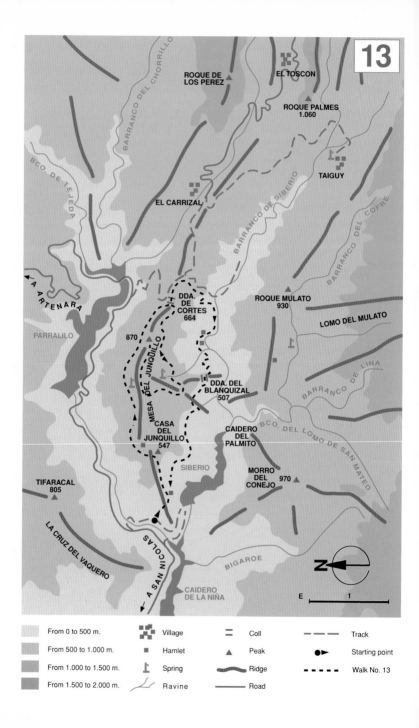

13

ROQUE DE LOS PEREZ

EL TOSCON

ROQUE PALMES 1.060

BARRANCO DEL CHORRILLO

BCO. DE TEJEDA

TAIGUY

EL CARRIZAL

BARRANCO DE SIBERIO

BARRANCO DEL COFRE

A ARTENARA

DDA. DE CORTES 664

ROQUE MULATO 930

LOMO DEL MULATO

PARRALILO

870

MESA DEL JUNQUILLO

DDA. DEL BLANQUIZAL 507

BARRANCO DE LINA

CASA DEL JUNQUILLO 547

CAIDERO DEL PALMITO

BCO. DEL LOMO DE SAN MATEO

SIBERIO

TIFARACAL 805

MORRO DEL CONEJO 970

A SAN NICOLAS

LA CRUZ DEL VAQUERO

BIGAROE

CAIDERO DE LA NIÑA

E 1

	From 0 to 500 m.	⊞	Village	=	Coll	---	Track
	From 500 to 1.000 m.	■	Hamlet	▲	Peak	●►	Starting point
	From 1.000 to 1.500 m.	⌇	Spring	∿	Ridge	▪▪▪	Walk No. 13
	From 1.500 to 2.000 m.		Ravine		Road		

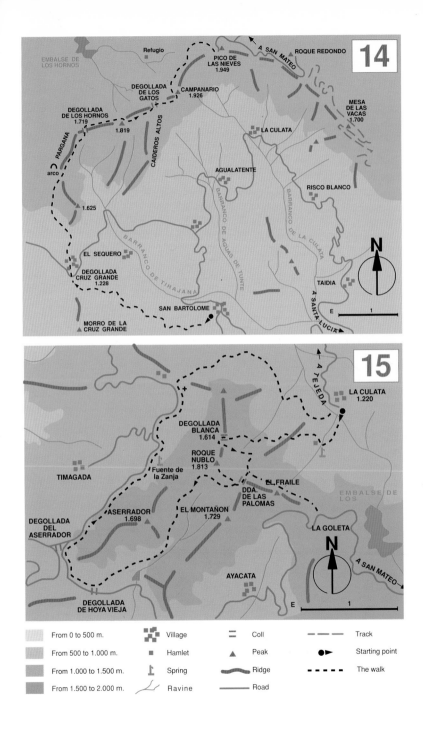

14

EMBALSE DE
LOS HORNOS

Refugio

PICO DE
LAS NIEVES
1.949

A SAN MATEO

ROQUE REDONDO

DEGOLLADA
DE LOS
GATOS

CAMPANARIO
1.926

MESA
DE LAS
VACAS
1.700

DEGOLLADA
DE LOS HORNOS
1.719

▲ 1.819

CAIDEROS ALTOS

LA CULATA

PARGANA

arco

▲ 1.625

AGUALATENTE

BARRANCO DE AGUAS DE TUNTE

RISCO BLANCO

BARRANCO DE LA CULATA

EL SEQUERO

BARRANCO DE TIRAJANA

DEGOLLADA
CRUZ GRANDE
1.228

SAN BARTOLOME

TAIDIA

A SANTA LUCIA

E   1

N

MORRO DE LA
▲ CRUZ GRANDE

15

A TEJEDA

LA CULATA
1.220

DEGOLLADA
BLANCA
1.614

ROQUE
NUBLO
1.813

TIMAGADA

Fuente de
la Zanja

EL FRAILE

DDA.
DE LAS
PALOMAS

EMBALSE DE
LOS

ASERRADOR
1.698

EL MONTAÑON
1.729

DEGOLLADA
DEL
ASERRADOR

LA GOLETA

N

A SAN MATEO

AYACATA

E   1

DEGOLLADA
DE HOYA VIEJA

From 0 to 500 m.		Village		Coll		Track
From 500 to 1.000 m.		Hamlet		Peak		Starting point
From 1.000 to 1.500 m.		Spring		Ridge		The walk
From 1.500 to 2.000 m.		Ravine		Road		

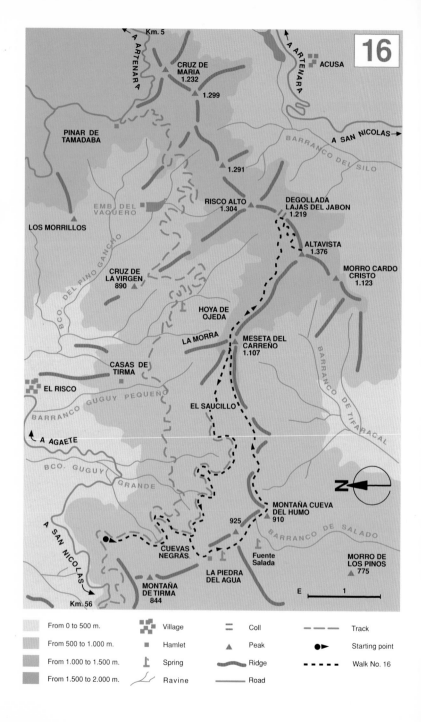

16

A ARTENARA Km. 5

CRUZ DE MARIA 1.232

1.299

A ARTENARA

ACUSA

PINAR DE TAMADABA

A SAN NICOLAS →

BARRANCO DEL SILO

1.291

EMB. DEL VAQUERO

RISCO ALTO 1.304

DEGOLLADA LAJAS DEL JABON 1.219

LOS MORRILLOS

ALTAVISTA 1.376

MORRO CARDO CRISTO 1.123

BCO. DEL PINO GANCHO

CRUZ DE LA VIRGEN 890

HOYA DE OJEDA

LA MORRA

MESETA DEL CARREÑO 1.107

BARRANCO DE TIFARAGAL

CASAS DE TIRMA

EL RISCO

BARRANCO GUGUY PEQUEÑO

EL SAUCILLO

A AGAETE

BCO. GUGUY GRANDE

N

MONTAÑA CUEVA DEL HUMO 910

925

BARRANCO DE SALADO

A SAN NICOLAS

CUEVAS NEGRAS

Fuente Salada

MORRO DE LOS PINOS 775

LA PIEDRA DEL AGUA

MONTAÑA DE TIRMA 844

E   1

Km. 56

From 0 to 500 m.	Village	Coll	Track
From 500 to 1.000 m.	Hamlet	Peak	Starting point
From 1.000 to 1.500 m.	Spring	Ridge	Walk No. 16
From 1.500 to 2.000 m.	Ravine	Road	

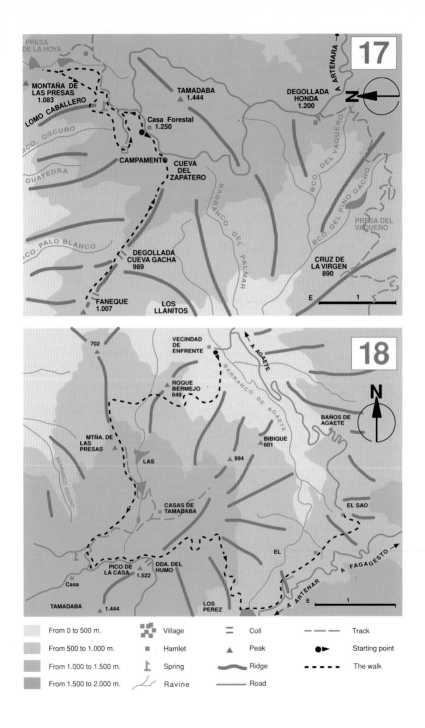

Map 17

PRESA DE LA HOYA

ARTENARA

17

N

MONTAÑA DE LAS PRESAS 1.083

LOMO CABALLERO

TAMADABA 1.444

DEGOLLADA HONDA 1.200

BCO. OSCURO

Casa Forestal 1.250

BCO. DEL VAQUERO

GUAYEDRA

CAMPAMENTO

CUEVA DEL ZAPATERO

BCO. DEL PINO GACHO

BARRANCO DEL PALMAR

PRESA DEL VAQUERO

BCO. PALO BLANCO

DEGOLLADA CUEVA GACHA 989

CRUZ DE LA VIRGEN 890

FANEQUE 1.007

LOS LLANITOS

E   1

Map 18

702

VECINDAD DE ENFRENTE

A AGAETE

18

N

ROQUE BERMEJO 649

BARRANCO DE AGAETE

MTÑA. DE LAS PRESAS

BAÑOS DE AGAETE

LAS

BIBIQUE 601

994

BARRANCO OSCURO

CASAS DE TAMADABA

EL SAO

PICO DE LA CASA 1.522

DDA. DEL HUMO

EL

A FAGAGESTO

Casa

TAMADABA 1.444

LOS PEREZ

A ARTENAR

E   1

From 0 to 500 m.	Village	Coll	Track
From 500 to 1.000 m.	Hamlet	Peak	Starting point
From 1.000 to 1.500 m.	Spring	Ridge	The walk
From 1.500 to 2.000 m.	Ravine	Road	

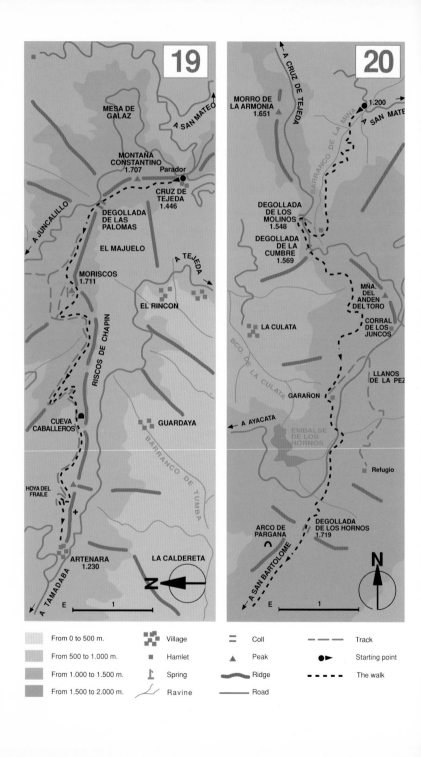

19

MESA DE GALAZ

A SAN MATEO

MONTAÑA CONSTANTINO
1.707   Parador

CRUZ DE TEJEDA
1.446

DEGOLLADA DE LAS PALOMAS

A JUNCALILLO

EL MAJUELO

A TEJEDA

MORISCOS
1.711

EL RINCON

RISCOS DE CHAPIN

CUEVA CABALLEROS

GUARDAYA

BARRANCO DE TUMBA

HOYA DEL FRAILE

ARTENARA
1.230

LA CALDERETA

A TAMADABA

E   1

20

MORRO DE LA ARMONIA
1.651

A CRUZ DE TEJEDA

BARRANCO DE LA MINA

1.200

A SAN MATE

DEGOLLADA DE LOS MOLINOS
1.548

DEGOLLADA DE LA CUMBRE
1.569

MÑA. DEL ANDEN DEL TORO

CORRAL DE LOS JUNCOS

LA CULATA

LLANOS DE LA PEZ

BCO. DE LA CULATA

GARAÑON

A AYACATA

EMBALSE DE LOS HORNOS

Refugio

ARCO DE PARGANA

DEGOLLADA DE LOS HORNOS
1.719

A SAN BARTOLOME

N

E   1

From 0 to 500 m.	Village	Coll	Track
From 500 to 1.000 m.	Hamlet	Peak	Starting point
From 1.000 to 1.500 m.	Spring	Ridge	The walk
From 1.500 to 2.000 m.	Ravine	Road	

You must follow the pipeline going North which runs along the base of the Montañon: the route is easy to follow until you reach some pine trees and orange groves (30 min.); a little past that point you have to watch the landmarks: the route gives the impression that it is going into the channel of the ravine but you should not do that; you should keep close to the left, close to the sheer wall, except when you meet a huge boulder which has come off the Montañón. It is an area with a lot of vegetation. Your route now becomes clearer and it goes up via steps through some rocks and brings you out on the flat very close to the channel until you come to plots of fruit trees; at this point you could miss the way but you should not gain height: instead you should keep as close to the channel as possible until you cross it through a bed of tall reeds (there is a clear trodden path through the reeds); this brings you to the track which goes up to the dam. You follow the track upwards, leaving on your left the guard's house and the shelter, till you reach the wall of the dam (903 m.–1 hr. 30 min.).

Once you have crossed the wall of the dam you follow out alongside a concrete pool for distributing water beside the overflow outlet of the dam, and at the end of that you ascend, on the right, the hill which has an electricity pylon/lightning conductor at the top: on your right you have left behind, in the bed of the ancillary ravine, a small dam. Along the hillside runs the track that goes from Cercados de Araña to the village called Lomo de la Palma; you have to take that track as far as the village (30 min.).

From the lower houses of Lomo de la Palma you can see the Soria dam and, on its left, blocking part of your view of the dam wall, the Risco de Agujero (Needle Rock), so called because it has a hole in its top. You have to take the ridge which heads for this rock, using the restored path; you pass the Southern face of the rock on the Paso de la Galana – and keeping close to the base of the road, this brings you into the Cañada (open ravine) del Almacigo at the point where it goes straight to the Soria dam.

When you reach the Soria dam you do not cross it: you

take a track to the left which passes a house surrounded by an iron fence and you descend via an original seam of volcanic rock towards other, semi-derelict, houses. (You must not go straight on the path which leads to another house higher up and to the open ground of Huesa Bermeja.) Our route leaves the houses on its right, and enters a lovely palm grove and then reaches the Fuente del Brusco, a spring set in a cave, with a little drinking pool made of cement (20 min.). You then retrace your steps and about twenty metres from the spring you descend via the El Brusco path which passes close to cultivated terraces (initially you leave on your right an iron fence, plain to see) and this leads you into the bottom of the Barranco de Arguineguín. It is a very nice route, through palm groves and lots of vegetation: it is popularly called the Ruta de la Fruta (the Fruit Route).

The path continues along the left hand side of the ravine, without crossing it; here there is water all the year round, the overflow of the Soria dam. There is a beautiful willow wood at this point. If we were to follow the ravine upwards, we would come to the containing wall of the dam – but that is not part of this Walk. Downwater, the route leads us naturally over to the other side of the ravine through tall reeds and wild willows (*sauces*) until it reaches terraces with fruit trees etc.; it descends gradually (for some stretches there are cement steps and handrails) until it reaches the track which comes in from the opposite side, at a point where there is a house and sheds for livestock (1 hr. 10 min.). Although you could get back to base by following this track (mentioned earlier as the one which leads to the lower houses of El Brusco) it would be too long and tiring because you would have to gain height again; so our route does not cross the gorge: it keeps along its left-hand side and descends through plots and past irrigation channels, along the bottom of the ravine until it reaches the houses of El Caidero and from here it is only one kilometre to the finishing-point (45 min.).

San Nicolás to Güi Güi Grande to Tasartico

• Ascent: 603 m. to the Degollada de Peñon Bermejo; then a descent to the beach of Güi Güi Grande; then an ascent of 547 m. to the Degollada de Aguas Sabinas • Time: 6 hr. 30 min. • Length: approx. 13 km. • Starting-point: At the 68.8 km. mark on the G-810 road from Agaete to San Nicolás, before reaching the latter town. You take a short tarmac road to the right, which brings you to a school • Finishing-point: the same • Difficulty: 3

The entire coastal area between La Aldea and Mogán, limited on the East by the road which links these two towns, is wild and rocky. There are a few points of habitation: the whole area is as if it was made by a gigantic plough which has left great furrows, separated by spikey ridges. Given the fact that there are no settlements of any importance, these mountains seem even more off the beaten track – part of another world entirely, designed for exploration and pursuit of the outdoor life. The area is almost a perfect triangle, with Amurgar and Los Picachos at its Northern tip, the Hogarzales on its Eastern tip and the Las Tabaibas and Aguas Sabinas on the South.

The ravines which descend from East to West are short ones, without a head or middle stretch, and they are cut at the Eastern end by the chain of the Cedro, Hogarzales and Vacas mountains and on the West by the coast, only three kilometres long.

The tarmac ends at the school (your starting-point mentioned above; 90 m.) and becomes an earthen track which you follow, up the right-hand side of the Cañada (or open ravine) de Vallermoso. You pass by (on your left and right) small res-

35

ervoirs, cultivated plots and isolated buildings, and you have to leave the track when you come to a biggish reservoir on the right on the side of which are marked the first white arrows which mark the way to Güi Güi. This is a very good bridle path and it brings you up steadily and steeply past channels carrying water from the dams on the Aldea ravine. When you are about 400 m. up, the path makes a big curve to skirt a deep, short subsidiary ravine which runs from the Picacho de la Cruz and brings you to a house beside a small reservoir (you can drink from the pipe that fills this reservoir; 1 hr.). A bit above this, to the left, and set back from the path, there is another house (a white building with a red roof). On the opposite side of the main ravine you can see the Picachos and Amugar, separated by the Degollada de Vallermoso.

A bit further on the path reaches the bed of the ravine and it follows up the ravine in a zig-zag as far as the Degollada de Peñon Bermejo (693 m.–1 hr.); it goes beyond the head of the ravine of the same name and heads South-West to the Degollada de Güi Güi Chico. From here you descend rapidly in ten minutes and then there is a fork in the route: the track to the left goes down along the bottom of the ravine as far as the Casas (houses) de Güi Güi Chico; the one going left, which is the one being followed on this Walk, continues on as far as the Degollada del Espigón (613 m.), which divides it from its neighbour, Güi Güi Grande. There are two points when you have to use steps cut into the rock (no difficulty involved).

There are spectacular views from all the colls, which are watersheds between the ravines; piles of rock dividing the ravines from one another means that the whole area involves lots of ups and downs.

Once inside the Güi Güi Grande gorge, the path descends gently towards the bottom of the ravine where there is a grove of palm trees and a number of cave-dwellings (an area known as the Media Luna), and the remains of cultivated plots, at the base of the Montaña de Hogarzales. The vegetation on the bottom of the ravine is fairly lush, with lots of palm trees, and you can hear the sound of water as it spills down the falls. You follow along the right-hand side of the ravine, where there are arrows and other marks done in white paint, until you reach a small empty reservoir surrounded by palm trees in the area known as Zamora (2 hr. 15 min.). From here you descend directly keeping parallel to the channel of the ravine, and reaching the beach in 30 minutes.

At the Media Luna you can take one or other of two routes – the one described in this Walk which keeps along the right hand side, and the other which goes down into the ravine, passing some rocks smoothened by the waters, and then goes down via steep steps until it comes out in a rather odd sort of tunnel of canes. The bottom is very overgrown – thick vegetation – but a tunnel about ten metres long has been made right through a thicket of high canes (you have to keep your head down to get through it); it is quite dark inside. Very soon after coming out of the tunnel you reach the reservoir referred to. This route back to base is much shorter than the one which goes along the side of the ravine, but you would need to be careful when you are making your descent. It is really better to be doing it in reverse, that is, using this route when you do the whole Walk in the opposite direction to the one described here; it saves you time.

Near the route, on the right, you can see 'stone roses', peculiar fluted rock formations spreading out from a single point in every direction, making a sort of star or flower. This phenomenon does not occur often on the island.

You return to Tasartico via the Degollada and the Cañada de Aguas Sabinas; it takes 1 hr. 30 min. and is fairly steep due to the amount of height you have to recover (there is a good path as far as the Degollada de Aguas Sabinas; it starts Southwards at the only house near the channel of the ravine: it is the only path going South, so you can't miss it.).

Variant: When you enter the Barranco de Güi Güi Chico you can follow the bed of the ravine up as far as the Casas (15 min. from the fork), ascending along the opposite side via a very nice path which goes up as far as the Degollada del Palo

(450 m.–50 min.) where you change over to the Barranco de Güi Güi Grande and go down to the reservoir via the Cañada del Telar (30 min.). On the way down you pass on your left an unusual cave with an entrance shaped in the form of a heart.

From the Casas of Güi Güi Chico you can go straight down to the beach by following the channel of the ravine, but it is a difficult descent. It is well worth while stopping at the Casas and enjoying the beauty of the place and the stone roses on a cliff on the opposite side of the ravine.

Los Azulejos to Montaña de las Monjas

• Ascent: 1,000 m. • Time: 6 hr. 15 min. • Length: approx. 14 km. • Starting-point: Los Azulejos; on the road from Mogán to La Aldea, at the 20.9 km. mark, 11 km. from Mogán, just past the Bar-kiosk in Los Azulejos • Finishing-point: the same • Difficulty: 0

At the sharp bend below Los Azulejos two ravines cross the road and join up a little further down: as you look at the mountain, the one on the left is the Barranco de Ojeda, and the one on the left the Barranco de los Palos. Our route begins just below an enormous boulder, twenty metres to the right of the channel of the Barranco de los Palos (470 m.) following the marking cairns: it twists up the side of the ravine, leaving the Caidero de la Menta on its right, and then it goes into the channel of the Barranco de los Palos, which it crosses at the level of the Charcos Azules. Ascending now on the other side (you are now above the Roque de la Galana) the path goes via the Llanos de la Bruma and the Los Palos cave (which it leaves on its right) and then once more it crosses the channel of the Ravine and takes you onto its right hand side. Here the path becomes much less steep and brings you gently through high pine trees; it is still marked out by cairns up to the point where it meets the forestry track; the last section of the route follows that old forest track which links up with a track 1,800 m. from the mountain refuge (930 m. –1 hr. 30 min.), which you reach in another 20 minutes. At the refuge you can get a drink of water from a tap opposite the door.

You have to follow the track in the direction of the Degollada de las Brujas, but then you leave it and take a path to the left, shortly after reaching a metal (green) water tank positioned to the right of the path; this path is a short-cut which saves you a kilometre and a half and brings you up onto the track again higher up: you continue along the track until you reach the Degollada de las Brujas (1,227 m.–40 min.): towards the West, about 200 metres up there is a spring; to reach it you have to go down as far as the first bend in the direction of the Casas (houses) de Inagua and take a path which leads straight to it.

At the Degollada de las Brujas you have to stay on the track for 100 m. going towards the Cruz de las Huesitas (see Walk No. 11), and then you leave the track, by going left and up a good stretch of mountainside which brings you onto the Montaña de las Brujas (1,409 m.), then descending into a small depression and ascending the Southern side of the Montaña de las Monjas (1,470 m.–45 min.). This peak has a twin sister to the East which is about ten metres lower; both are splendid vantage-points for seeing the Northern zone of the Sandara–Inagua chain. The drops to the North and West are spectacular – the Lina, Cofre, Bigaroé, Siberio, Pino Gordo and other ravines.

You then have to go back as far as the Montaña de las Brujas and at a little coll below its peak you take a path going East (it is not in great shape); this brings you on to the track a little before the Degollada del Agujero (1,318 m.) which you reach in 30 minutes.

You now go down the South side of the mountain, that is, take the track East and 50 metres further on you leave it and take a path going to the right which in 45 minutes brings you to the Pino de la Hora, very close to a pine cone dryer. The Pino de la Hora is a cross-roads located 200 metres to the West of the cone dryer; at this point begins the track Southwards along the ridge which you have to take and which will bring you down to the mountain refuge in 40 minutes; there is no problem about finding the way; it is well marked; it goes via the Llanos de Ojeda and ends up parallel to the channel of the Barranquillo del Salobre at a metallic notice which reads 'Monte de U.P.–Inagua'.

You cross the track you used for your ascent, and the bed

of the Barranquillo and then you go up through a rocky area, where there is a metal post which marks the beginning of the way down; it is beside a pine tree and an area where the water runs through a channel; from here on you cannot lose your way: there are cairns all the way to the road and the route is well trodden; it goes through Los Quemados and goes down along the ridge towards El Roque, which you can see ahead of you all along this route (until you reach the road (387 m. – 45 minutes). It will take you another 20 minutes on the tarmac to get back to where you started.

This Walk can be shortened by just going as far as the Aula and taking the downward path from the track; or else by going up to the Degollada del Agujero and descending from there, without going up the Montaña de las Monjas.

Inagua

• Ascent: 781 m. • Time: 6 hr. 10 min. • Distance: approx. 14 km. • Starting-point: Degollada de La Aldea. At a point 14 km. from San Nicholás on the G-810 road to Mogán • Finishing-point: the same • Difficulty: 0

The Degollada de La Aldea or de Tasarte (642 m.) is a natural vantage-point which gives you fine views of the Barrancos de La Aldea and Tasarte; it is a compulsory stop on the road between Mogán and San Nicholás. Across from the bar, beside a big road sign which marks the turn for Tasartico, a path starts out in a North-Easterly direction (it is well marked), along the right-hand side of the hill; it soon changes direction completely, heading for San Nicolás, and it gradually makes its way to a flat stretch located about half way up: you go along the whole length of this flat part. In 25 minutes you reach a good specimen of Canarian pine alongside which there is a cross with the date 28.VI.77 in memory of someone deceased. The track is clean and well looked after and it only takes you an hour to get to El Laurelillo. You do not go as far as the track which leads down from the Casas (houses) de Inagua: your track goes off to the right, Southwards, and takes you to the base of the Inagua rocks; here it divides into two and you must take the path going right; this brings you soon to the spectacular Tasarte 'platforms' (*andenes*), and you go along them until you reach the Castillete (1 hr. 10 min.); this is a rock 1,163 m. high, located on Los Quemados; it has a TV booster on the top beamed towards Tasarte.

Alongside the Castillete there is a little coll carrying the path coming down from the mountain refuge of Inagua, but that is not the route we are taking; we are taking an arm which leaves the same coll and goes North along the flank of the

Montaña de Ojeda (you cannot mistake the way); you get to the Degollada de Las Brujas in 20 minutes; as you go, you leave on your left a number of kilns formerly used to extract tar and make charcoal from the wood of the pine forest. Some of these kilns are in a fairly good state of preservation: you can see the kiln proper where the wood was burned under slow heat, the container underneath for catching the tar or resin, and the little channel linking the two. These pine forests were over-exploited at one time but now they are well on the way to recovery.

In Las Brujas you take the path to the left going up the Montaña de Ojeda (1,363 m.); this leaves, below it, another path which ends up at a spring which is never dry; you reach the summit (you cannot lose your way) and from there you go on to the Montaña de Inagua (1,423 m.–45 min.), where you will get magnificent panoramic views of the Güi Güi mountains, the Barranco de la Aldea and the Montaña de Las Monjas right beside it.

It takes you 20 minutes to make your way back to the Degollada de Las Brujas (you are descending all the time along the track for 1.5 km., in a Westerly direction towards the Cortijo or Casas de Inagua, until you come to a big water deposit on your left (20 min.), which is set virtually in the channel of the Barranco de las Casillas. Just before the water deposit you leave the track and take another excellent path to the left which goes behind that structure and round the Montaña de Inagua until it brings you to your route down, just before the Tasarte platforms begin (50 min.). You descend to where you started out from; it takes an hour.

Variant: Hoya de los Poleos

Once you are on the Degollada de Las Brujas there is a nice walk which involves going round the Montaña de las Monjas via the Hoya de los Poleos. You follow the track Eastwards (towards the Cruz de las Huesitas), and you reach the Degollada del Agujero in 30 minutes. From here two paths descend on the North side: you must take the one on the left which goes down into the bottom of the Lomo de San Mateo. The path zig-zags down; you have to leave it once you get to the channel of the ravine (you are on the left hand side), at a point where there are some cairns: then you slowly go up the left-hand side of the ravine, diagonally through an area where there is a lot of vegetation and you reach the Casas de Inagua (you can't lose your way.) (1 hr. 30 min.) At first you go up the side of the ravine and then the path goes down, crossing the heads of the Barrancos de Bigaroé and Garabeteras; when you reach an old corral for livestock, it goes off right and goes down to a short offshoot off the track to the Casas de Inagua: you follow this until you reach the houses. You cannot mistake the Hoya de los Poleos: there is a distinct menthol smell which comes off the 'Poleo de Monte' which is covered with huge shrubs, so big that they can make passage difficult.

Very near the houses there is a pool of drinking water fed by a pipe; you reach this via a short track going West, which runs between two other tracks: the lower one ends up near the Casa de los Peñones, on the West flank of El Viso; and the higher one (which is the one you take now) brings you to El Laurelillo and links up with the track which brings you down to the Degollada de la Aldea.

Morro de Pajonales and Morro de la Negra

• Ascent: 400 m., with various ups and downs • Time: 5 hr. • Distance: approx. 9 km. • Starting-point: 3 km. from Ayacata on the way to Tejeda, there is a turn to the left towards El Toscón and El Juncal. As soon as you go onto this side road, you have to take the left fork, which is the way to El Juncal. The path of the Walk leaves the road 700 metres from the turn, just before a sharp right-angle bend; it goes off to the left • Finishing-point: the same • Difficulty: 0

From Roque Nublo a long ridge runs off in a South-Westerly direction. For 14 km. it divides the two great channels of Tejeda to the North and Ayacata-Mogán to the South. Most of this ridge is located in the Reserve of Ojeda, Inagua and Pajonales. It is one of the best places for views in the whole island. This Walk uses a recently restored path and it is very easy to recognize where the path begins.

From the road which goes down to El Juncal (1,300 m.) you ascend along the left-hand side, under the Chirimique Rocks, which are to the East. At the watershed you continue along the ridge going South-West, avoiding the little pinnacles (you are at 1,400 m.); some of these are to the North, others to the South. The path continues via the Morro de los Almacenes as far as the Montaña de los Jarones (1,491 m.), which you reach in 50 minutes. You are now at the Eastern limit of the National Park. You have to descend 170 m. to the Degollada Blanca and then go up the Morro de Pajonales (1,434 m.), which is a little bit off to the right (to ascend the Morro you have to leave the path for a minute); this stretch takes another 50 minutes. From the peak of the Morro you can see (below you, to the North) the Casa Forestal (forestry station) de Pajonales and (very close to the summit), a number of open spaces cleared of stones which formerly were used when tar and charcoal were manufactured here; there are still the remains of kilns used in centuries past.

It takes you 20 minutes to go down via the mountainside called the Lomo Picón, which brings you to the point where tracks intersect (1,223 m.), known as the 'Cruz de Las Huesitas'; the track going towards the North leads to the Casa Forestal de Pajonales and El Juncal; the one going South, to the Las Niñas dam via Nameritas; and the third goes into the National Park. Our route takes this third track and leaves it a few metres from the chain that blocks the passage of vehicles: you take a path to the left (a very good one) which ascends to the upper part of the Lomo de Hierba de Risco. This path follows the Southern side of the Morro de la Negra and keeps going on, right through the Park, but our Walk leaves it when it reaches the coll between this *morro* and its neighbour, 'Solapones de La Carnicería'. Once on the coll you go East, ascending the mountainside right to the top of the Morro de la Negra (1,450 m.), along a safe, open ridge (50 min.).

Some 35 minutes more and you are at the Cruz de los Huesitas again, having taken a path which descends diagonally to the track via the Northern side. Twenty minutes on from where the tracks cross, you reach the Casa Forestal – and it takes another half an hour to get to El Juncal. From there you have to take the metalled road to get to your starting-point (45 min.).

A large part of this walk is through the pine forest; it is a good idea to bring water with you because there is none to be had at any point on the route; and it is also a good idea to wear strong footgear in order to avoid falling and slipping on the pine needles which carpet the mountain side, especially in the steep descent from the Morro de Pajonales.

Mesa del Junquillo

• *Ascent: 750 m.* • *Time: 6 hr. 15 min.* • *Distance: approx. 12 km.* • *Starting-point: The 'Presas' (dams) road, 9 km. from San Nicolás de Tolentino on the way to Artenara* • *Finishing-point: the same* • *Difficulty: 3*

Up above the back of the Caidera de la Niña reservoir, on the road from San Nicolás to Artenara (called the 'Presas' road) a track goes off to the right leading to the Siberio dam. On the other side of the road there are some derelict buildings which were used when the dam was under construction (275 m.).

The Walk begins by going down the track towards the channel of the Barranco de La Aldea; you go over via a bridge across which there is a chain to prevent vehicle access. Some 300 metres from the bridge, on the left, you can see a glen or open ravine (*cañada*) through which the path ascends (cairns mark the route); this brings you right up as far as the watershed with the Barranco de Siberio. When you reach the ridge you can see the dam over on the other side (25 min.) The path goes to a derelict house made of cement blocks, which it leaves on its right, and it continues to be clearly marked as far as the Casa del Junquillo (547 m.–35 min.), located at the Western base of the Mesa del Junquillo (from where you have views of both ravines).

At this point the most spectacular part of the Walk begins: the route keeps on to the left, along the side of the Barranco de La Aldea, which is fairly level, skirting the sheer walls which sustain the copula of the Mesa, at a level of 600–700 metres. It is an exposed but safe route, well marked, well trodden; from it you can see the 'Presas' (dams) road and the wall of the Parralillo dam 400 metres below; there are lots of rushes (*juncos*) on the route on account of the wetness at the base of

47

the Mesa (from which it takes its name). About 25 minutes on from the Casa there is a permanent spring of water beside the track at a place always in shadow. The path meets the trail coming up from the bottom of the Barranco de La Aldea that starts below the tunnel through which the Presas road runs. You follow the trail as far as the Degollada de Cortés (664 m.– 40 min.).

On the Degollada de Cortés you leave the trail and take a path to the right which (without losing height) runs along the Southern face of the Mesa until you reach a prominent spur which goes off from the Mesa southwards. This trail is worse than the one which brought you up, but it presents no difficulty. When you reach the spur you begin to gain height, going up a short series of steps to a cave in which there is another spring; it goes on along a platform (*andén*), changes to the other side of the spur and takes a turn to the right. Here the path disappears: you have to go up on the right to a big cave, and then you turn and go South; then you turn again, to the right, and go to the highest part of the plateau of the Mesa. When you reach the plateau of the Mesa you continue Eastwards up to the cairn at the top (870 m.–1 hr.), a great vantage-point for seeing the Barrancos de Tejeda and Siberio and the great peaks of Altavista, Pajonales and Sándara. As you go up, you should make a mental note of the houses at the bottom of the Barranco de Siberio and the track which leads to the Degollada del Blanquizal, because you will be passing along there later (they are easy to see from high up).

Your return route involves going back the way you came as far as the Degollada de Cortés (1 hr.).(There is another, very tricky, route down via the Western spur of the Mesa as far as the Casa del Junquillo, but it is not part of the plan for this Walk.) You follow the track going towards El Carrizal: when you reach a fork at a bend you take the track to the right (which leads to the channel of the Barranco de Siberio) until you come to a bend where the earth is red (15 min.) and here you leave the track and take an excellent path which runs along a mountainside and brings you to a ruined house; you stay with it, it goes to the right and crosses a small ravine via a containing wall, and then it crosses the ravine again, in the opposite direction via another wall and descends into the channel of the Barranco de Siberio (there is water here all the year round). Very soon, a bit further down the ravine, you take a cut-stone path which leads to some houses and cultivated plots; when this path divides in two, you should take the leg going to the left until you get to the house lowest down, 'the German's house' (350 m.–30 min.).

When you reach the houses of Siberio you should be careful because at first the path is not very clear; but it very soon gets much better. You leave the German's house on your left, going up along a terraced plot and then you immediately turn to the left towards the channel of a small ravine in which there is a waterfall (normally dry) chalky white in colour; the path crosses the ravine, going to the left and, amid lots of vegetation, you reach the path that brings you up to the Degollada del Blanquizal (507 m.–35 min.). From here the path continues on the same level until you reach the house made of cement blocks which you saw as you were making your ascent (1 hr.); it is not a very good path but you won't lose it if you keep your eyes open and you don't lose height.

From that house to the point where the Walk started, it is only a matter of 20 minutes.

San Bartolomé to Pico de las Nieves

• Ascent: 999 m. • Time: 5 hr. 30 min. • Distance: approx. 16 km. • Starting-point: San Bartolomé de Tirajana • Finishing-point: the same • Difficulty: 0

Leaving San Bartolomé via the North side of the football pitch (950 m.; see the end of Walk 20) we meet a restored path which runs along the Northern flank of the Morre de la Cruz Grande until it reaches the road that leads to Ayacata and Tejeda in the enclave known as Cruz Grande, very near the start of the forestry track; you take this track, going South through the pine forest of Pilancones (1,228 m.–1 hr.).

Crossing the main road you take another path that goes to the right of the white houses and this brings you easily to the Degollada de los Hornos, from where you have a view of the Roque Nublo on the uppermost part of the Barranco de Tirajana (1,700 m.–1 hr. 30 min.). The path is in a good state of repair, with excellent stonework; it runs first along the side of the Tirajana ravine and then goes through the channel of the Barranco de Chira via a platform at the base of the rocks. On your left are the small Cho Flores dams and a fine cave where you can spend the night if you want to, in the 'Pargana' area. Before reaching the Degollada it is worthwhile making a deviation to the left to see the curious natural stone arch located on the edge where you get a view of the Barranco de Meca (see Walk 20). When you reach the watershed on the Degollada de los Hornos and get your view of Roque Nublo, you turn East, taking a path between pine trees which goes via the Degollada del Campanario de los Gatos and the base of the Campanario and the Degollada (1,926 m.) and leads directly to the Pico de las Nieves (you do this in an hour, without leaving the ridge). You can easily reach the peak of the Campanario

50

by going off to the right and then dropping back on to your path.

To get back to where you started, you can take the same route in reverse (2 hr.). There are other ways down to San Bartolomé de Tirajana not described in this book: one goes down via the Mesa de las Vacas as far as Taidía; the other is via the Cañadón del Jierro, which brings you as far as La Culata; in both cases you have to walk on the main road for a few kilometres to get back to where you started.

Roque Nublo

• Ascent: 580 m. • Time: 4 hr. 20 min. • Distance: approx. 9.5 km. • Starting-point: La Culata (Tejeda) • Finishing-point: the same • Difficulty: 0

The tarmac road that goes to La Culata (1,220 m.) ends up in a small plaza which has a car park; the Walk starts here, in the street which climbs up the hillside. Very soon you take a concrete path to the right which leads into the bottom of the Ravine (we are at the head of the Barranco de Tejeda) and brings you to the other side across a bridge. The path goes up past the highest houses, running alongside the pines, and it brings you into the Barranco de la Casa del Pino. A bit further on it leaves on its left the Casa del Pino (a ruined house) and a spring which in the very bed of the ravine, a few metres above the spot where the path crosses the ravine. It then goes up the other side of the ravine, bending as it goes; it changes on to another little ravine and brings you to the Degollada Blanca (1,614 m.–1 hr.) where the paths intersect; the path to the right goes round the Nublo via the North, but this Walk takes the path to the left, which brings you in 30 minutes to the easiest track for access to the Nublo, from La Goleta, at the base of the Roque del Fraile. It then goes on to the right, passing via the Roque del Gallo, the Degollada de las Palomas and the Tablón del Nublo until it reaches the base of the Roque.

Roque Nublo is the great symbol of Gran Canaria. Its slim outline features in tourist and commercial literature. It is a gigantic monolith, of very hard rock, suitable for rock-climbing; it is the eroded remnant of a huge lump of volcanic agglomerate. It forms part of a volcanic area known as 'Roque Nublo' which seemingly originated in enormous volcanic explosions which destroyed the centre of Gran Canaria three or four million years ago.

To return to the Degollada de las Palomas you take the path going East, which descends between pines until it crosses with the path coming up from the North side from the Degollada Blanca, and then it goes on to the left to enter the basin of the Nublo Ravine; it takes you across the bottom of that Ravine, onto the left-hand side, and then further down it goes over to the right-hand side, leaving on your left a small dam; then you go down zig-zag to a water deposit and the 54 km. mark of the road from Tejeda to San Bartolomé, on the Degollada de Hoya Vieja (1,400 m.–1 hr. 30 min.). On your right you have passed El Aserrador and before your last descent you can see the sharp-pointed Roque Betancuria beside the main road. All along this part of the route you can see the remains of buildings and abandoned plots – a long enclosing wall, terraces and caves.

You go along the road for about three kilometres in the Tejeda direction (35 min.), passing by the Degollada del Aserrador (from where a road branches off to El Juncal and El Toscón) until you reach the start of a big, gradual bend to the left; here starts the well-made path (*camino real*) which you take to get back to La Culata. The point at which this good path starts is easy to find because it is just to the right of some houses and beside a signpost for Roque Nublo. Your route takes you at first up along a wide cement path to the Cruz de Timagada, a lovely little spot with the Cross set on a base of red cut stone; it dates from 1915 according to an inscription on the base. Around 3 May each year the Cross is covered with flowers which people leave as a sign of devotion to the holy Cross: up to the late 1960s there was a church feast-day of the Triumph of the Cross on that day, and devotion to that feast is quite widespread in the Canaries and especially in the Tejeda area.

It takes 30 minutes to get back to La Culata. The path is in a very good state of repair and it runs right along the side of the hill, about half way up, giving you a good view all the time into the Tejeda basin. There are wonderful views of the Roque Bentayga, and the Nublo towers on the other side 500 metres above.

You can, if you want, take a longer route beginning your walk at 'Cuevas Caidas', 910 metres up, and two kilometres from Tejeda; from there a path begins which links up with the path we have just described.

There are a number of other routes you can take around the Roque Nublo, following *caminos reales* (public paths) recently restored: the simplest (a half hour's walk) is to go from La Goleta on the road from the Llanos de la Pez to Ayacata. Another is to begin on the Degollada de la Cumbre (Walk 20), going down to La Culata, then up to the Nublo and returning to your starting-point via the Los Hornos dam, Garanón and the Andén del Toro. You could also walk up from Ayacata to La Goleta via the Barranco del Nublo to the Degollada de la Hoya de la Vieja, and return to Ayacata via the road.

Altavista

• *Ascent: 663 m.* • *Time: 5 hr. 45 min.* • *Distance: approx. 15 km.* • *Starting-point: at the 56 km. mark on the road from Agaeta to San Nicolás: you take an earthen track to the left for two kms.* • *Finishing-point: the same. You can also end this Walk on the road from Artenara to Pinar de Tamadaba at the 5 km. mark* • *Difficulty: 1 (the stretch to and from the Artenara road: 0)*

After you pass the 56 km. mark on the G-810 road, between Agaeta and San Nicolás, there begins the access track to the Tirma townland and its mountain. Of the four practical ways to enter this area, the one chosen here probably has the best views. The track hugs the northern side of the Montaña de Tirma and is accessible by road as far as the 7 km. mark on the road which runs round the Tamadaba pine forest; however, in order to go the whole way along this track you need to get special permission from the Authorities of the island; if you do not have this permit, you can take your vehicle as far as a house called La Portada, leaving it at the chain which blocks your way, at a point two kilometres from the main road and 674 m. up above sea level.

At this point you begin your walk, following the forestry track for two kilometres, and then you leave it by going to the right in a Westerly direction, using another track which is in a bad state of repair and which brings you to the Cuevas Negras; here you get your first sight of the green-and-red-grained rock which is so typical of the area and which has been used in the construction and decoration of many important buildings on Gran Canaria. A small spring feeds a pool very near the Cuevas Negras, in the area known as 'La Piedra de Agua'. Your route now goes straight to the ridge/watershed between the Tirma region and the Barrancos de Salado and Tifaracal (or Chof-aracal), and you stay on this ridge really until you reach the top of Altavista.

The Montaña de la Cueva del Humo (910 m.) is the first peak you meet and then you go on via the Montaña and the ridge in an Easterly direction, going up and down the short steep hills until you reach the restored pathway from Artenara to San Nicolás. This path takes you into the Hoya del Escobón passing onto the Northern side (left as you ascend here) of the Lomo del Cura, the ridge which descends from Altavista; it passes the Hoya del Laurel and goes up the Paso del Palo to take you to the Degollada de las Lajas del Jabón, the coll which separates the two most important peaks in this massif – Altavista (1,376m.) and Risco Alto (1,304 m.). Here you leave the main path (which goes to Artenara) and veer to the right (South West) and go up in a zig-zag as far as the top of Altavista ('peak with good views'). It is not easy to find a better name for this peak: the sheer drops on the Acusa side, the Parralillo dam and the Barranco de Tejada are impressive, and your view extends South to La Cumbre, Tejada, Artenara, Acusa and the Roque Nublo and Bentayga. On the West lies the Tamadaba pine forest, and to the North the many ravines which cut across Tirma as far as the town of Risco and its beach. In fact this mountaintop has two peaks, the Easterly one a metre higher than the other, but it is worth while taking a look at both. This Walk takes 3 hours 15 minutes so far.

Your descent follows the same way as you came up, as far as the Hoya de Ojeda, where you should look for a second forestry track to the right which ends up at the Hoya, a bit above the area known as 'El Saucillo', and which runs parallel to the track you used going up but on a higher level. This links up with that lower track and brings you back to your original starting-point; a considerable part of it is cut out of veins of green rock. It takes 2 hours 30 minutes to descend.

You can end this Walk on the Artenara –Tamadaba road, at the 5 km. mark, but if you do that you need to have transport organized to take you back to your base.

You can get to Altavista in an hour and a half by setting out from the point mentioned in the previous paragraph: after passing the 5 km. mark, on the left, there is a cairn of stones beside a pipeline (1,160 m.); here a fine path starts which brings you straight to the summit. This is a walk anyone can do; it goes through pine trees all the way, and has the advantage of keeping to the ridge the whole time, giving good views of both sides.

WALK NO. 17

Tamadaba to Punta Faneque

• Ascent: 460 m. • Time: 3 hr. 45 min. • Distance: approx. 9 km. • Starting-point: the 11 km. mark on the road which runs round the Tamadaba pine forest • Finishing-point: the same • Difficulty: 1 (the last stretch after the Cueva Gacha: 3)

At the 11 km. mark on the road that runs round the Tamadaba forest, you find the Casa Forestal (forestry station;1,250 m.) beside a parking area laid out with picnic tables and stone seats. Almost in front of the Casa a path begins, heading West, parallel to the main road but on a lower level; it goes for some 300 metres to an earthen track beside a stone building with a chimney (a place for burning waste). Very close to this, beside the path, which is clear to see, is the Cueva del Zapatero, a natural cave, neat, clean and whitewashed. The path descends in a zig-zag from in front of the cave; you cannot lose your way because it is very well marked and in a good state of repair; it goes almost all the way along the mountainside, which ends at the Punta (or Risco) Faneque.

Faneque is a huge spur three kilometres long which thrusts out Westwards from the Montaña de Tamadaba, its level ridge being about 1,000 m. high. The drops on both sides, all the way along, are very sheer. For 1.5 kilometres you descend between pines down the mountainside which is hereabouts quite open, until you reach the Cueva Gacha (989 m.) where a spectacular ridge begins – not one recommended for people who suffer from vertigo. The ridge is solid underfoot and in-volves no risk, but the drop on either side is nearly 1,000 m., so you feel rather exposed. You have to scramble at one point for five metres, but no difficulty is involved. The Punta or Risco itself (1,007 m.) is inaccessible from the ridge: before you

58

reach the peak the ridge is broken suddenly by a drop with sheer 50 or 60 m. walls (impossible to negotiate).

On the other side there are huge boulders which uphold the top of the ridge, which has the form of a platform. All along this part of the route you in front of you, in the distance, Teide (the highest mountain on Tenerife island); it takes an hour to do this stretch. On your left – to the South-West – you can see the whole Tirma basin and the beach and town of El Risco; over to your right is a unique view of Agaete and the Puerto de las Nieves with a series of parallel Ravines stretching down from Tamadaba – the Barrancos de La Palma, Palo Blanco, Guayedra, Oscuro and Altavaca.

You return the same way as you came (there is no alternative); it takes an hour and a quarter to reach the Casa Forestal. You can make this a longer walk by taking the circuit I now go on to describe; this route gives you a fairly complete conspectus of the North-East side of the massif, and it provides breathtaking views.

From the Casa Forestal you go North along the road (where you reached with your vehicle); you take the turn that heads for the Campamento (camping site) and you leave the tarmac road when you reach a sharp bend beside the car park. If you go up the earthen track, you come to the Reventón fountain dedicated to John Doorly, an Englishman, but then you should go back to the main track. Shortly after passing the barbeque area and its tables, you go down to the left along the *camino real* (recently restored) which, further down, crosses a drain designed to channel lthe rainwater to the Tamadaba dam. You follow the *camino real*, going to the right, Northwards, which brings you to the dam (1,050 m.–40 min.).

You come back as far as the drain and shortly after you pass the point where it crosses the track, it is worthwhile to leave the path and go about 150 metres to the right in order to look down into the Barranco Oscuro and Agaete. There are walls here equipped for practising rock-climbing.

Then go back to the path-drain and stay on it until you reach the Campamento (1,180 m.–30 min.); the path rises very gently along the top of the Barranco Oscuro. It takes 20 minutes to walk from the Campamento to the Casa Forestal, whether by the main road or along the water pipeline which runs from very near the Campamento to the Casa Forestal.

Ruta de la Rama

• *Ascent: 1,150 m.* • *Time: 6 hr.* • *Distance: approx. 9 km.*
• *Starting-point: Vecindad de Enfrente* • *Finishing-point: the same* • *Difficulty: 0*

As you go up the Barranco de Agaete ('El Valle') a turn to the right, after three kilometres, leads to the villages of San Pedro and Vecindad de Enfrente (one is on this side of the ravine, the other on the 'opposite' side). Your path begins at this second village (200 m.) just before the tarmac road ends, to the left of a lovely house standing under a big eucalyptus tree; it runs between the low walls of various farms, crosses an irrigation channel and brings you to the eucalyptus. This is the route taken by people who go up Tamadaba in Agaete's traditional 'Festival of the Branches [*Ramas*]'. They walk up during the night, carrying torches, to collect branches from the pines and bring them back down the valley.

A bit further up you cross another irrigation channel (no longer in use) and you go straight along the Lomo de los Balos, which is a watershed. You continue along the hillside (you are in the Ingenio ravine), passing some abandoned terraces and a pair of nicely proportioned palm trees; you cross the bed of the ravine and veer right – in an ascent until you reach the very visible caves of an aboriginal granary or store for animal feed set in the rock side (1 hr.). You cannot lose your way on this whole route because the path is clearly marked and in a good state of repair. In the bed of the ravine, beside the path, you will meet a spring, the Fuente de las Goteras.

On your left you have passed the La Quesá and La Rajá rocks, and a bit further below on the left, the Agujereá rock – so named because there is a hole through its top like the eye of a needle. On some sides of this rock there is as sheer 400-metre drop.

61

After passing the caves you go through a zone of volcanic scree and you come out behind the Roque Bermeja (649 m.) on whose peak there is a cross which looks down on the village you started out from. You are now in the Bibique or Berbique district where there is a circular stone threshing-floor in which the grain is cleaned which is harvested in the cereal plantations of this neighbourhood. You leave the Maria Ravine on your right and you walk parallel to a waterpipe which comes from the Tamadaba dams and goes as far as the Montaña de las Presas, which you go round from behind (this brings you to the Presa de la Hoya)–1 hr. 20 min. Another way of going up to the dam (quicker but steeper) involves taking a path to the left a little after you cross the channel of the Barranco de Maria and going up as far as the wall of the dam almost parallel to the pipeline.

When you come to the dam, you find a branch of the track on your right flanked by two rows of svelt pines; if you take that track, in about ten minutes you meet some abandoned plots where there are big chestnut trees and fruit trees of various kinds and some very large and very ancient oak trees.

After you pass the dam, you have to leave the path and go off to the right, and you meet it again a little higher up at the place laid out for picnics and barbeques (there is a spring there too) and this immediately brings you to the road which runs round the pine forest (1,250 m.–30 min.). You follow the road going East (to the left) as far as the Degollada del Humo on the watershed, where the path starts that descends as far as the Perez dam. When you come to a junction, lower down, you take the middle path (North-East), which descends gently (the one to the right is a short-cut, but it is not recommended). Further down there is another junction: the path to the right goes down to the Lugarejos dam and the one to the left, which is the one you should take, goes to the Perez dam via the Barranquillo de Cho Gregorio (1 hr.).

You have to cross the containing wall of the dam until you reach a house; from here, for five minutes, you have to go along tne road linking Coruña and Fagagesto and then you leave the road and descend on the left in the direction of El Hornillo and El Sao (630 m.): you soon see a clear, well trodden path. Throughout your descent you pass on your right many inhabited cave-houses and two good springs.

From the dam to the road which goes up via Berrazales it takes one hour ten minutes and then you have a further hour of descent via the road or via the disused path in the channel of the ravine, before you reach Vecindad de Enfrente.

Moriscos

• Ascent: 325 m. • Time: 2 hr. 30 min. • Distance: approx. 8 km. • Starting-point: Cruz de Tejeda • Finishing-point: Artenara • Difficulty: 0

This route can be defined as a fine walk along a spectacular ridge: it involves no difficulty at all and consists of a gentle ascent as far as the top of 'Los Moriscos' (or, on some maps, 'Las Moriscas') and then an easy stroll down along an excellent forestry track to Artenara. Half is through pine trees. The route runs parallel to the road linking the Parador de la Cruz de Tejeda and Artenara, but on a higher level.

Behind the Parador (1,446 m.) a well-marked path leads to a cement watertank leaving an electricity transformer on its right. Above the tank a the path ascends through shrubs and some pines, initially following the line of high tension wires. It then continues on the flat along the side of Tejeda until you reach a very good vantage-point (with parking) beside the main road on the Degollada de Las Palomas (30 min.). On the peaks to the right you can see radio aerials (Montaña Constantino), and way down below you on the left various rocks and needles (Riscos de Chapín).

From the vantage-point on Degollada de Las Palomas the path goes on, following the ridge and the pines until you come to a track which turns left and bring you up to Los Moriscos in 40 minutes (1,771 m.). There are buildings and a white disk aerial at the very top, very close to the cairn which identifies this peak as a triangulation point. On your way up you have had marvellous views of the whole Caldera de Tejeda (a vast crater); and from the top you can see the ravines, ridges and mountains of the North, with the Montañón Negro in the foreground. You have walked through the Northern part of the huge horseshoe of the *caldera*. The vertical walls which ring the crater are volcanic 'dykes' belonging to a conical system of dykes whose centre would be to the West of Roque Bentayga. The prevailing geological theory about the origin of the crater is that a huge volcanic mass was eroded, leaving exposed walls or dykes of rock more resistant to erosion.

The Walk continues by descending along the track as far as the 'Paso Blanco', where you find the stone cross (you go to its left) and you stay on this track until you reach Artenara. In 20 minutes you come to a huge needle of rock beside a cave cut out of the rock – the Cabelleros caves: it is worthwhile going down to the base of the rock and peering over the precipice which falls sheer in the direction of the village of Guardaya, in the Tumba ravine, 600 metres below.

You can make rapid progress on the track and in 30 minutes, going down all the time, you come to an intersection; here you have to go straight ahead (not taking the turn to the right which goes down to the main road). When the track ends, you then descend by a restored path which brings you to the Cruz de Toril. There you take a path to the right (there are steps and a wooden handrail) which goes past houses to the shrine of our Lady of La Cuevita (1,270m.–30min.), which is well worth a visit. Popular devotion to the Blessed Virgin has found here an expression which it is difficult to equal, as can be seen from the work the local people have done to build this shrine and maintain it. The route ends in Artenara (you must have planned in advance how to get back to your starting-point, which is 15 kilometres away by road).

You can plan a shorter way by starting at the Parador and going to Moriscos and then going back the way your came; or else by going straight up to the top of Moriscos via a track which starts 5.5 kilometers from the Parador on the road to the Caldera de los Pinos de Gáldar. If you do this Walk going in the other direction, that is, starting at Artenara, you should give yourself 40 minutes more, because there is more climbing involved.

Barranco de la Mina to San Bartolomé

• Ascent: 519 m. • Time: 6hr. • Distance: approx. 12 km. • Starting-point: where the G-811 road from San Mateo to Tejeda crosses the La Mina Ravine, near Lagunetas • Finishing-point: San Bartolomé de Tirajana • Difficulty: 0

This route runs North-South across the central cupola of the island, and almost all of it is along old paths which have recently been restored. It is a favourite route of hill-walkers, and in earlier times was much used by the original inhabitants of the island, by muleteers and by conquistadors.

The route begins at the bridge that crosses the waters of the Barranco de La Mina (1,200 m.); there is always a flow of water in the channel, which explains why there is plenty of vegetation, especially big willow trees. It continues along the left- hand side of the ravine, leaving some houses on your left, and it takes you across the channel of the ravine to the other side and brings you all the way up to the higher road.

The ascent is steep and long and there are many branches off to the right which lead to waterfalls and pools which are well worth exploring (but then you have to retrace your steps to get back to the main path). The path goes up the side of the ravine in a zig-zag through abandoned terraces which are now used by campers. In spite of all the efforts made to keep this area clean, you come across a lot of litter and rubbish, especially in a cave on the upper terrace on which (as well as other caves) there is a derelict house.

Your path, which is not along the water channel but rather parallel to it, above it, brings you to a cluster of houses (there is a grain mill on the opposite side). You could continue your ascent via the path which leads to the houses, but our route takes you on without crossing the channel of the ravine, bringing you to a big open cultivated area where there are some byres for livestock and two lines of tall chestnut trees. Underneath one byre beside the ravine there is a gallery of fresh water and at that point you take the earthen path to the right (direction West) which brings you to the main road from Cruz de Tejeda to Cazadores and Los Pechos on the Degollada de los Molinos (1,548 m.–1 hr. 15 min.), a good point for viewing the Caldera de Tejeda.

On the coll (*degollada*) you continue along the watershed going South, following a well-marked path which comes from Cruz de Tejada and leads to the Degollada de la Cumbre in 20 minutes (1,569 m.); there is a very nice house right on the coll. This point is where the long *camino real* (public path) from the mountain top meets the branch which descends as far as La Culata de Tejeda; it is very easy to see where the *camino* starts as it has recently been restored. The *camino* leading to the top takes you along the West flank of the Montaña del Andén del Toro passing by the Corral de los Juncos (40 min.), a forestry house which you leave on your left. The path crosses a small ravine and involves a short ascent up to a path intersection: you should continue straight ahead (not take the branches which go off to right and left); this means you go through the pine trees of the Llanos de la Pez to the track leading to a camp, the Campamento del Garañón (30 min.). Facing the metal gate at the entrance to the Campamento, a path leads down between two stone walls and brings you to the Los Llanos de la Pez road in 15 minutes.

Your route follows the road for some 450 metres in the direction of Ayacata; it brings you on the left of the Barranquillo de Juan Francés, towards the South, by a clearly restored path at a point where there is a placard put up by the environmental authorities; the path brings you to the Degollada de los Hornos (1,719 m.–30 min.) where it changes direction and starts going down. (See Walk 14.) After you have gone for ten minutes, it is worthwhile to deviate to the right down a gentle mountainside (covered with pines down lower and bare on the upper part) to investigate a curious natural stone arch which is a kind of window looking out onto the Roque Nublo. As you go to the coll, half way up, take a look back to see the huge green pine forest on the Llanos de la Pez.

Once back on your downward route, you keep going (you can't miss the way) along the Llanos de Pargana, leaving on your right the small Cho Flores dams as you make your way down on a curving route as far as Cruz Grande (1,228 m.–1 hr. 30 min.) where there are houses and a Calvary. You have to go down to the road in order to take, on the very bend, a track which has a cable across it preventing vehicle access; after you pass the first bend to the left you meet up with the stone-paved path which takes you to San Bartolomé. Just before the first houses of the town there is a line of huge Canarian pines. You keep going down, along the tarmac road, until you get to the parish church (887 m.–1 hr.).

Mountains in Order of Height

Mountain	Height in metres	Height in feet	Walk No.
Pico de las Nieves	1,949	5,941	14
El Campanario (Puntón Agugereada)	1,926	5,870	
Roque Redondo (Alto del Canario)	1,919	5,849	
La Calderilla	1,840	5,608	2
Roque Nublo	1,813	5,526	15
Cruz del Saucillo	1,800	5,486	
Mesa de las Vacas	1,783	5,436	
Moriscos	1,771	5,398	19
Montaña de la Retama	1,709	5,209	1
Montaña Constantino	1,707	5,203	19
El Aserrador	1,696	5,169	15
Roque Saucillo	1,690	5,151	1
Montañón Negro	1,662	5,068	
Montaña de las Arenas	1,575	4,801	1
Sándara ó Azandaras	1,570	4,785	
Morro de la Cruz Grande	1,539	4,691	
Roque El Pino	1,523	4,642	
Lina	1,518	4,627	
Montaña Barreto	1,509	4,599	
Roque Grande	1,507	4,593	
Peñón de la Arena	1,506	4,590	
Risco Blanco	1,502	4,578	
Caldera de los Marteles	1,500	4,572	2–3
Yescas	1,500	4,572	
Pinos de Gáldar	1,500	4,572	
Los Jarones	1,491	4,545	12
Monjas	1,468	4,474	10–11
Morro de la Negra	1,450	4,420	12
Carnicería	1,446	4,407	
Tamadaba (Pico la Bandera)	1,444	4,396	17
Morro de Pajonales (Morro Picón)	1,434	4,371	12
Morros de las Vacas	1,433	4,368	

Mountain	Height in metres	Height in feet	Walk No.
Roque Bentayga	1,412	4,304	44
Inagua	1,423	4,337	11
Brujas	1,409	4,295	
Pino de San Antonio	1,406	4,285	
Morro del Barranquillo del Agua	1,381	4,209	
Altavista	1,376	4,194	16
Montaña de Ojeda	1,363	4,154	11
Guanil	1,323	4,033	
Morro de Hierba Huerto	1,319	4,020	6
Risco Alto	1,304	3,975	16
Atalayón	1,254	3,822	
Espigón (Meseta de Valsequillo)	1,250	3,810	2
Tauro	1,214	3,700	7
Risco de las Tunas	1,164	3,548	
El Castillete	1,163	3,545	10–11
Trujillo	1,149	3,502	
Amurga	1,131	3,447	4
Talayón – Roque Almeida	1,107	3,374	4
Puntón de la Solana	580	1,768	
Lomos del Garañón	530	1,615	6
Peñón Bermejo	518	1,578	

Recommended Reading

Araña y Carracedo, *Los volcanes de las Islas Canarias* (1980). Ed. Rueda, Madrid (in English and Spanish); on the volcanoes of the Islands.

Bramwell, D. and Bramwell, Z.I., *Flores silvestres de las Islas Canarias* (1987). Ed. Rueda, Madrid. (There is an English edition.)

Kunkel, G., *Diccionario botánico canario* (1991) Edirca, Las Palmas de Gran Canaria. (There is an English edition.)

Santana Santana, A. et al., *Guía de senderos de Gran Canaria*, 2 vols (1994) Cabildo Insular de Gran Canaria, Las Palmas de Gran Canaria.

Cardona Sosa, M., *Rutas Canarias* (1996) Canarias 7. Las Palmas de Gran Canaria.

Martinez Garcia, J., *Rutas de montaña. 50 itinerarios por Gran Canaria* (1993). Mapfre Guanarteme, Las Palmas de Gran Canaria.

Geografía de Canarias, 2 vols (1993). Ed. Prensa Ibérica, Las Palmas de Gran Canaria.

Maps available in specialized bookshops.

Servicio Geográfico del Ejército, scales 1:25.000 and 1:50.000, Cartografía del Cabildo Insular de Gran Canaria. Mapa Geológico de España.